OUT OF MY LEAGUE

OUT OF MY LEAGUE

Dr. Bernie Kastner

iUniverse, Inc.
Bloomington

Out of My League

Copyright © 2011 by Dr. Bernie Kastner.

All rights reserved. No part of this book may be used or reproduced by any means, graphic, electronic, or mechanical, including photocopying, recording, taping or by any information storage retrieval system without the written permission of the publisher except in the case of brief quotations embodied in critical articles and reviews.

iUniverse books may be ordered through booksellers or by contacting:

iUniverse
1663 Liberty Drive
Bloomington, IN 47403
www.iuniverse.com
1-800-Authors (1-800-288-4677)

Because of the dynamic nature of the Internet, any web addresses or links contained in this book may have changed since publication and may no longer be valid. The views expressed in this work are solely those of the author and do not necessarily reflect the views of the publisher, and the publisher hereby disclaims any responsibility for them.

Any people depicted in stock imagery provided by Thinkstock are models, and such images are being used for illustrative purposes only.

Certain stock imagery © Thinkstock.

ISBN: 978-1-4620-2373-8 (pbk)
ISBN: 978-1-4620-2375-2 (ebk)

Printed in the United States of America

iUniverse rev. date: 05/25/2011

CONTENTS

To my Mom and my brother Ron

CHAPTER ONE

THE OTHER LEAGUE

The last two seasons were good ones. I batted .521 and .444 respectively. The level of pitching wasn't that tough, but I never admitted it to my family and friends. I was also a very lenient scorer. I remember one play where we had a runner on first and I lined a sharp single up the middle. The center-fielder gobbled it up and threw a perfect strike to the shortstop covering second base thereby forcing the runner out. I still scored it as a hit. After all, the runner should have beaten the throw. Why should I be penalized for someone who runs like a turtle? There should at least be some reward for being out on the field every Sunday at eight a.m.

We played on grass fields at a time when most jocks were still sleeping or were just about going to sleep. A motley crew of guys from Avenue N would show up sporting beards, half beards, some with their tzizis (fringes) hanging out, and those who wore black socks with cut-down dungaree shorts. Yet others didn't bother combing their hair, and some were chain smokers. Every once in a while one of us would bring down a ringer who didn't wear a yarmulke.

We played seven-inning double-headers and it was always a choose-up game. After a while, the less athletic among us would get the message after not being picked for the fourteenth straight time and would eventually not show up anymore. There was, however, one who remained despite the most obvious hints like "your mother is calling you", or "we don't have any extra gloves". If that didn't work, we'd make him an umpire. And that's when the fun really began. He would say "strike one, I mean ball one, no no no strike one—yeah that's it, it was a good one right on the inside part of the plate". Then the batter would complain: "But it was a foot over my head!" One week he came down with a cast on his arm—and expected to play. We didn't even let him ump.

Each game was amazingly different from the next yet ironically I couldn't help but get that déjà vu feeling week after week. I never knew there were so many ways to make errors. Just when you've seen them all, oops, there goes another one between the legs of the pitcher, the short center-fielder, the center-fielder, the center-field fence, the dog walking beyond the fence, and through the legs of the old lady walking the dog.

I wasn't on the losing end of these games all of the time; but somehow it wasn't fun being on the winning end of this ordeal either. Sure we'd have a few good laughs, like the time the catcher squatted down behind home plate and ripped a gaping hole under his crotch. Or the time one of the guys took a vicious swing at the ball whereupon it rolled three feet up the third base line. Instead of running to first, the runner just stood there incredulous that the ball didn't go beyond the part of the grass where his pot belly stuck out. Meanwhile the pitcher got to the ball and promptly sailed one over the head of the first baseman and down the right-field line. Seeing this, the batter took off for first and then headed for second. The right-fielder, huffing and puffing, whipped the ball toward second base. The ball hit the shoulder of the runner and deflected into left-center field (the ball, that is). Now halfway to third, the runner realized that he had missed touching second base. He turned around heading toward second while the left-fielder picked up the ball and fired it to the second-baseman. It went off the tip of his glove and out toward the right-field line. The runner headed for third. This time the right-fielder couldn't even make it to the ball as he tripped over a rock and ripped up the skin on his knee caps. The first baseman tracked the ball down as the runner eyed home plate. Then came the throw, the sliiiiiiiiide . . . . OUT!

Three times per game of this and it wasn't funny anymore.

One good thing, though, about this no-pressure, non-competitive environment was that if you screwed up, nobody cared. No statistics were kept, nor articles were written about you, and most would not remember whether you went 0 for 4 or 2 for 4 the previous week. I can't say no one noticed though. To the pitcher who threw two straight grounders to home plate one could hear "come on, this isn't bowling for dollars", or "last night you were high", and "you're so low the curb gets more respect than you".

The right-fielder, who, trying to nail a runner at home plate, once chucked the ball clear over the backstop and into someone's backyard. He would then hear "A little higher and you would have bumped off that bird", or "that's what I like about you—you make plays at the plate *so* exciting".

Being all members of the same tribe eased the sting of such comments; it was like being part of one big happy family. Actually, it was refreshing to be brought down to earth where it was easier to keep our inflated batting averages and egos in check.

If that didn't work, then our annual "all-star" game against the local Italians quickly brought us to our senses. This was an event arranged each summer between us Jews and "them" usually via two colleagues who worked at the same firm. The event took place on our home field—not that that made much of a difference. In case of a rumble, we wouldn't have stood a chance.

One major problem in preparing for such a game was who to tell and who not to tell. Since all twenty who showed up on a regular basis were paid up participants (to cover the cost of equipment), who decides who plays and who doesn't? Well, there were really only five or six genuine ballplayers among us in our "league". The rest were selected by the guy who arranged the game. Those selected were sworn to secrecy regarding the time and date of the game. If the game was held on a Sunday morning, we would publicly cancel that week due to some excuse such as lack of interest.

I was the starting shortstop for us and believe me if I tell you that I had not been so psyched for a game since my little league days. The game represented a mixture of fantasy and reality—it's the local all-star game - the best neighborhood Jewish ballplayers versus the best local Italian ballplayers. Or simply put—the Jews vs. the Italians, period. There was no love lost between us and it showed, albeit in a civilized manner.

I built this game up in my mind to emotional levels that were beyond reason. For all those times as a kid growing up in a mixed neighborhood in Brooklyn and being on the receiving end of name calling and ridiculing, now it was payback time in a controlled setting where personal confrontation was not an issue. Here was an opportunity to show them their place, humble them for the moment, shut them up for once.

It was a glorious thought, and I would savor the moment (in my mind). Each night for days before the game, I would lie in bed, close my eyes and dream up fantastic plays I would make in front of 50,000 fans...*Second and third, two outs for the Italians, bottom of the ninth, the Jews up by one run. Big Joe Vitano at the plate. He already is 2 for 3 in the game including a home run. The count runs to 2 and 0. The pitch. Lined hard in the hole at short—OH WHAT A CATCH! The shortstop for the Jews dives to his right and makes an incredible back-hand play. And the Jews hold on to win it 4-3. The shortstop is being mobbed by his teammates—the fans are going wild...*

Finally the day arrived. It was a scheduled double-header to start at 9am. We got there at 8am for practice—Lord knows we needed it. Surprisingly enough, though, we looked good. We took our fielding practice as we rotated taking swings at the plate. At 8:55am the Italians began to show up. My heart began to beat faster. Some of them looked like they just woke up. Another came with girlfriend in tow, and yet another two showed up each carrying a handle of an ice box full of beer. The rest of the team machoed their way onto the field—it was already 9:20. They took the field for their warm-ups. Their infielders were burning the ball back to the first-baseman—such arm strength I haven't seen since sitting at field level at Shea Stadium about 15 years ago. They looked scary. What if one of their throws comes off line just as I'm running out a grounder—it could hit me in the head!

We were anxious to get the first game going, so we convinced them not to take batting practice (Jewish minds at work). Since they were the visiting team, we took the field first. I scooped up a warm-up roller from our first-baseman cleanly, but my throw didn't reach him. It bounced about two feet in front of him, kicked up some dust, and rolled out to short right-field. A confidence-builder all the way.

We agreed that the team up at bat would provide an umpire to call balls and strikes and to call the bases. This prevented anyone from complaining that the ump is one-sided. Before I could get a chance to restore my confidence on being able to reach first base, the umpire shouted "okay, let's start". Now I'm thinking 'please don't hit the ball to me for the first six innings or so'.

The first batter, Vinnie, their second-baseman, stepped to the plate. He was about 5'10", muscular, and wore a sleeveless undershirt and sawed-off dungarees. He cocked the bat high above his shoulders and presented a sharp closed stance at the plate. Despite the closed stance, I sensed that he was a pull hitter so I played deep in the hole at short. He lined the first pitch hard down the right-field line. So much for my intuition.

The next two pitches were low and outside. By now my concentration was acute, while desperately trying to remain loose. The next pitch was hit sharply—a two-bouncer past the third-baseman's outstretched glove and ticketed to left-field for a single. I took two quick steps to my right and lunged a backhand at the ball. I managed to snare it in the webbing of my glove trying to keep the momentum from taking me into the visiting dugout. I planted my feet firmly and then uncorked an overhead bullet to first. When I let go, I thought the ball would sail over the first-baseman's head. But I was practically at the edge of the outfield grass when I released the throw so it came in at eye level to the first-baseman. The throw beat the runner by half a step. It was truly a beautiful play to watch. Almost as good as my fantasy. But this was real and it was exhilarating. We immediately earned some respect—for the moment at least.

The next batter hit a lazy fly ball to center which was caught for the second out. Then their number three hitter lined the first pitch right between my eyes. Fortunately, I stuck my glove between my face and the ball. We had survived the first inning.

In the dugout we were slapping each other high fives and giving out pats of approval on each other's backsides. We didn't get blown away in the first inning. The unlikely feeling that we could beat these guys suddenly came upon us.

In our half of the inning I led off. Batting left-handed against a right-handed pitcher, the count ran to 2 and 2. I grounded the ball slowly toward shortstop, but by the time the ball got to first, I was already by the bag for an infield hit. Our next batter forced me out at second. We didn't score that inning or in any other inning for that matter. The only scoring came in the top of the sixth inning. Their second-baseman, the one with the sleeveless shirt, doubled to right-center. The next batter popped out to first and the following hitter grounded out to second, moving the runner to third. We had a reasonable chance to get out of the inning unscathed when their number four hitter smacked a routine grounder up the middle within my reach at short. As I extended my left shoulder to go down for the ball, the ball hit a rock and crossed clear over my opposite shoulder and into left-field. The game saw no further scoring. As always, it was tough to lose 1-0. The second game, by comparison, was anti-climactic—we won 6-2.

Thus went the annual summer all-star classic. After the game, there was general goodwill, but they were somewhat disturbed over the fact that we won the second game.

One week remained until the end of the summer season. The turnout on the softball diamond was good because everybody was back from summer vacations and each wanted to get just one more swing in before the weather turned cold. The usual crew showed up and once again the game started in grand fashion with the "who is going to choose who" debate:

"I'm not going to choose."

"I don't wanna choose."

"I suck—so how can I choose?"

"I don't know the players well enough so I can't choose."

"I always choose—I don't feel like it this week."

We may as well have gone home with such enthusiasm bubbling over.

Finally the suspense was too much for me and I chose somebody. Then the game started. Pop fly to second base—he's under it—he has it lined up—sticks up his glove—and the ball falls five feet behind him. Man on first and no outs. Next batter hits an easy two-hopper to third. He fields it cleanly, throws to second for the force play, but the ball sails over second base and into right-center field. One run scores. The batter pulls into second base as the throw comes in from right-field. The next batter lines a single to left field. The ball reaches the fielder on one hop, but he can't handle it. The runner from second scores and the batter winds up on second base.

And the merry-go-round continued. Errors, errors, errors. I couldn't take it anymore. I had to play a game where errors were not always the deciding factor. It had finally taken its toll. I needed a change. Maybe my good friend Gerald's team could use someone for next season.

CHAPTER TWO

GRAINY BEACH HERE I COME

During the fall and winter months my mind was preoccupied with hockey, basketball and football. Occasionally I'd give some thought to next spring's softball season and where I'd be playing. One day in February 1985 it hit me to start planning and set myself up with another team. I kept in mind Gerald's casual offer to look into joining his league, but didn't want to pursue it yet because for some reason I was unsure of playing in a serious competitive league. I was obviously putting off this decision. Maybe I was intimidated by the thought of not playing for fun. In a no-nonsense league I would be forced to perform under pressure. I kept saying to myself 'who needs the pressure on weekends? I have enough of that all week between family responsibilities and work'. And thus I couldn't come to grips with myself on this issue.

Suddenly, though, a brainstorm swirled down upon me. Ben, one of the guys in the choose-up league, bought a house on Staten Island and he once mentioned to me in passing that he would like to import me from Brooklyn onto a new team he was forming out there. Now here was a league, somewhat competitive, containing members of the same tribe, and I still might be able to play shortstop. I called him that evening and asked him if it wasn't too early to think about joining his league.

"There's a problem", he said. All team players must be paid up members of the community center".

"So, that's no problem", I said, "I'll become a member".

"But you see, the new team I'm forming is a second team from the center. The word got out and I may have to give preference to those who are already members."

"When will you know for sure?"

"Well, we're supposed to have a meeting right around spring break—I'll let you know then."

Two months passed by and I could no longer wait for Ben to call me. I was just about to pick up the phone to call him and the phone rang. It was Gerald. He said he met a guy at a league meeting who was forming a new team and needed players.

Gerald was one of my closest buddies. We grew up together on East 55th Street in Brooklyn, went to the same elementary school and hung out a lot during our high school and college years, even though we attended different schools. He always said what was on his mind and loved to put me in my place by showing me how much I really didn't know about things, especially girls. He made himself into the block's authority on the art of picking up a girl.

He loved retelling the story about going out with Rosie Winter, someone whose morals were rather loose. She had a twin sister Toni and one Saturday night she didn't have any particular plans to go out. When Gerald came to pick up Rosie and learned than Toni was also available, he decided to stay in that night and hang out with the both of them in their bedroom, while their parents were watching television in the next room.

As a sixteen-year old at the time, this was considered steamy stuff in our neighborhood.

Gerald gave me the name and number of the guy who was forming this new team and said that if I wanted to join the team I would have to let the guy know by the end of the week. I hemmed and hawed and transmitted ambivalence about it. But I could vacillate no longer. I called Ben from Staten Island.

"Any word yet?" I asked.

"We still didn't have the meeting. I guess we won't be having one for another two weeks."

"Two weeks?"

"Why, what's the matter?"

"Well, I just got this call from another league and they made me an offer to play provided I commit myself by the end of this week."

"What league is it?"

"It's called Grainy Beach. They play in Brooklyn on Sunday evenings at 6pm. It's a real league—no foolin' around. I just don't know if I want to get myself involved. I'd rather play with you guys. I'm giving you first crack." As if I was doing him a great favor.

"Listen, there's nothing I can do to promise that things will work out for you with my new team. I wouldn't want you to pass up the other opportunity and then find out you couldn't play with us either. Besides, at least the games at Grainy Beach won't be filled with errors".

"But I kind of enjoyed it, know what I mean?" I was just making up more excuses.

We ended the conversation with the clear understanding that I had to make a decision and not have the decision made for me. The time had come for me to grow up. Finally I shrieked 'okay, okay, I'll do it'. I still had some lingering worries like I wouldn't know anyone on the team, it was an untested flat-out risk involving a major time commitment, and most of all—could I handle shortstop in this new league?

The more I wondered about my ability to play well in this new league, it occurred to me: *will* I play shortstop? Maybe there will be somebody on the team better than me. I called the new team captain to introduce myself and to find out the answer to my question.

"Hello, Lenny?"

"Yeah, this is he".

"I'm the guy who Gerald from the red team recommended to you."

"Who?"

"You know, Jerry from the red team (he was called Gerald by close friends only). You met him last Friday night at a league meeting and told him you are looking for some players."

"Oh yeah, yeah. What position do you play?"

"Shortstop."

"Good, good. I got some pretty decent guys—some who played in this league last year, but mostly new guys."

"So what are my chances of playing shortstop?"

"Well, we're having some practices coming up and I'm gonna take a look at everyone at each position. If you say you play well, you have a good chance of getting it. You will be competing with one other guy so far, but he could also play third."

"Fair enough. When is the first practice?"

"This coming Sunday at 1pm at P.S. 114."

"Where's that?"

"Corner of Remsen Avenue and Glenwood Road in the courtyard. We should be getting a close look at what we look like so far. I expect a good turnout so come early. And don't forget to bring seventy dollars in cash plus two photo ID cards for our files."

I hung up in a pensive mode. Lenny's speech was deep and obviously Brooklynese. Didn't sound much like a team manager to me, but it wasn't fair to judge him on the basis of one phone conversation.

As compulsive as I was, I wanted to make especially sure that nothing kept me from coming on time to the first tryout at one o'clock. I set my alarm for 5:30am just in case I should oversleep. I couldn't eat anything the whole morning. I had forgotten to take my glove out of the car and into the house overnight. My glove was twenty years old and it had rips on the inside where the fingers go into the slots. The rips were such that through the dirt and rain and other kinds of weather it has stormed, it created a very hard and sharp edged dry feeling to the hand instead of that smooth silky leathery comfortable feeling. After sweating in it during a game, the ripped leather softened up a bit and made it bearable for the bare hand. I considered buying a batting glove and wearing it on my left hand to protect it from the rough interior, but the only time I went to the local sporting goods store, they didn't have my size.

I ran out to my car and fished out my glove from the trunk. It was a cold, blustery day and the rigid leather felt like it was going to crack into bits and pieces. I carefully placed the glove on the living room radiator cover—but no heat was coming up at the time. Actually, my glove was an amazing piece of, uh, cowhide. It stood the test of time very well. I remember putting rubber bands around it to create a pocket when I first brought it home. When that wasn't doing the trick, I'd sit on it. But once the pocket was established, it was like a vacuum cleaner. It made me look good on the field.

Years ago when my father signed me up in Amity Little League at age eight, I was a standout. I started out as a pitcher—to my knowledge I was the only ambidextrous pitcher to be found in those days. I didn't flaunt it, though, except once four years later, I was forced to show off by my coaches. It was in June of 1969, and I was the starting left-fielder for the Amity Little League all-star team. I had insisted on not pitching because of chronic pain in my arm(s) after a game—so the coaches, knowing a good arm (or two) when they saw one, suggested I play the outfield.

We were scheduled to play three or four exhibition games before actual competition began. It was a very good idea because the league rulebook dictated that if you lose just one game, you're out of the competition. Hey, the Brooklyn championship was at stake here, ya know?

One of the teams we played was not in this particular round of competition—they were called MQH, or Mary Queen of Heaven. It was a scheduled six inning game and at the end of five innings they were winning 9-1. They had a super pitcher who threw darts at us. We were totally outclassed. Perhaps because of this, I don't know for sure, our coaches decided to zap it back to them in a way in which MQH may go away as winners, but we (at least our coaches) would walk away proud nevertheless. They wanted me to pitch.

We got our last licks in the top of the sixth and we went down without scoring. Technically, the game was over since it was set for only six innings. But our coaches told us to take the field in the bottom of the sixth, and asked MQH to come to bat just one more time just to complete the inning. I was instructed to take the mound. I really didn't want to. They pleaded with me to do it—they wanted to show me off.

I began to warm up right-handed. I was disgusted that we were down 9-1, and I didn't understand why I had to pitch at this point. Years later I appreciated the coaches' thinking—I would probably have done the same had I been the coach.

The first two batters to face me popped up and struck out respectively. As I got ready to face the next batter, one of the coaches came out with my lefty glove.

"Here", he said, "let's show 'em a thing or two".

"Aw come on, do I really have to?"

"I want to see the expressions on their faces."

I then began warming up left-handed. I looked toward the other dugout. MQH's coach stood there with his hands folded and with exasperation said:

"What, another pitcher? What's going on here? Wait a minute, that looks like the same pitcher as before. Is it? It is! I can't believe it!"

The batter stepped up to the plate. I fired. Strike one! I could hear the MQH coach and our coaches wowing simultaneously. The next pitch was hit weakly on the ground to first base for an unassisted putout. One, two, three, and I walked off the field. That is, I tried. Before I could finish shaking hands with my coaches, the MQH coach and assistants swarmed around congratulating me with amazement at what I've done. I cherished the moment as best a 12-year old could.

Lenny, my new team's manager in the Grainy Beach League, called to check if I was going to show up. By this time I was really psyched. I had to put on four layers of clothes to keep warm, yet at the same time have mobility on the field; the temperature was hovering around 40 degrees with a wind chill factor that made it feel colder. I turned on the heater in the car and made my way toward Canarsie, about a twenty minute drive from my house. It seemed a lot longer though—I was howling at every red light, each slow poke driver, and every stop sign. At Flatlands Avenue I turned left onto Remsen Avenue then took the first right onto Glenwood Road and up one and a half blocks to the courtyard of P.S. 114. I slowed down and saw four guys throwing a ball around. Only four guys? I was sure I would be the last to show up. I found a parking spot and made my way toward the guys through the glass-laden, lopsided concrete yard.

As I drew near I wasn't noticed as their backs were toward me. Then one rather tall, baby-faced guy wearing dungarees and a jogging suit jacket turned and saw me coming. I opened up the conversation:

"Hey, you Lenny?"

"Yeah, Jerry's friend?"

I nodded.

"I dunno what's happenin' here—more guys were supposed to show up by now."

"How does the team look—at least on paper?"

"Well, I wouldn't say we have a bunch of ringers, but we have some decent guys. I have some guys coming down from Jersey, a friend of mine who plays on the Stuyvesant High baseball team, and one or two guys who played in this league last year."

"Sounds good. Lemme throw the ball around—it's getting cold standing in one place."

It turned out I was the last one to show up that day. I took grounders at short and fielded most of what was hit to me. My throws were not on target, but it was the first outing and it was only 42 degrees out there. But who's making excuses?

Here's a roundup so far of those who showed up:

Lenny pitched batting practice. He just turned 22, graduated from Brooklyn College and was working for a small accounting firm in the city. He seemed committed to putting together a good team, but didn't impress me as having the authority and organizational skills to really pull it off.

Stevo reminded me of Rick Cerone, a former major league catcher. Maybe it was no coincidence that he became our starting catcher. He kidded around a lot and ribbed his younger brother Nick whenever he could. Stevo also couldn't stop talking about a girl named Amy, who had more curves on her body than Sandy Koufax had on his breaking pitch. He described her as a perfect "10" and envied Tom, the guy she was going out with. Tom didn't show for practice.

Nick had some kind of face on him—even his profile was embarrassing. About 5'8" very thin with long straight hair, there was no question in my mind that we weren't members of the same tribe. He would try to befuddle Stevo with putdowns, but he usually didn't stand a chance.

At first base was Lenny's brother, Ned. He looked like an intellectual - sporting wire-rimmed glasses, he had a quiet air about him. He wasn't too swift on the field though. I later learned that he only showed up for the sake of practice—he wasn't trying out for the team. I guess he was pretty swift after all.

In center-field was fleet-footed Curt. A high school kid at a local Catholic school, he liked number 29 for some reason. Maybe it was his life ambition to become 29 one day. He certainly had a long way to go. Fair complexion, light hair, beady eyes, rubicund of visage. And he could sure get 'em in center.

We each took turns at bat. Unfortunately for me I couldn't take a full swing batting left-handed because part of the school building (with a low roof) was only about ninety feet away from home plate. Any pop up and the ball was lost. Left-field was no haven either; the fence was about fifteen feet high but only the bare poles remained. Any ball hit on the ground or over the left-fielder's head travelled past a small playground and right onto Glenwood Road. Right-center field was rather dangerous—it was a garbage disposal area for the school. Aside from the fact that it gave off a foul odor, the dumpsters were practically sitting in short right-center field. Hardly an ideal ballfield under any circumstances.

Somehow, though, I completed the practice with restored confidence. I was pleased with my fielding and knew that I would be in good form once the season started. After about two hours, we called it quits for the day. Lenny called me over and asked me for my pictures and seventy dollars. When I told him I didn't have it yet, he asked me to bring it to him next Friday night, the deadline for teams to join the league. I hadn't really committed myself at this point to be on the team, since I wanted to see what I was getting myself into. I told him I couldn't bring it to him Friday night, but perhaps another night. I didn't tell him that I usually spend Friday nights at services in the synagogue. Based on the first practice, it didn't look promising but it did offer a different look that might turn into something interesting. About the only thing to look forward to so far was Stevo's enthusiasm for Tom's girlfriend Amy. It may be worth it to show up just to see what develops.

Meanwhile, the Passover holiday came and the spirit of the holiday was refreshing. Preparations for the holiday in terms of cleaning, extra food shopping, and arranging schedules for family to be together for the Seder meals were quite taxing though. Aside from the religious aspects of Passover, the holiday brought in a glimpse of spring, as the warmer weather stared to show itself from time to time.

Since we had all recognized that the field basically stunk, in every sense of the word, it was suggested that the next practice would be either at South Shore High School or at the church parking lot on East 86th Street. We decided to meet at the church since it was closer and assured us that nobody else would figure on playing there before we arrived that Sunday morning.

Well, we were right—nobody else got there before us except for about two hundred cars that completely filled the lot. When I arrived, nobody from the team was there—so I drove to P.S. 114. It was empty. I wasn't early so something was going on. Exasperated, I drove to South Shore High School but nobody was there. I drove back to P.S. 114—still nobody. I even called Lenny's house and his mother just said that he left about twenty-five minutes ago and should be at the field. Of course she didn't know which one.

I drove around the block and by the time I pulled into a spot I noticed Lenny standing all alone in left-field.

"Did you just get here?" I asked.

"A few minutes ago".

"I guess we just missed each other earlier. So where is everyone?"

"I'm really ticked off. I spoke to the guys and they all said they'd be on time. Can't depend on them for nothin'. They were probably out drinkin' all night."

In an attempt to take his mind off being angry for the moment, I asked:

"So, the busy season is coming to a close for you, right?"

"Yeah. I've been working pretty hard lately—some weekends too."

"What's your last name?" I inquired with some trepidation.

He paused for a moment, and then hesitatingly answered "Steinberg".

"No kidding! You're Jewish?"

"Yeah", he said with his head down.

"I'm Jewish too. It's good to know there's another member of the tribe on the team."

"Yeah, well, the league is about 50-50 Jewish and Italian."

"Really? From what I've seen and heard so far I didn't think the percentage of Jews in this league was so high."

"Well, it seems to be mostly Italian. But there are definitely Jews in the league."

"Any others on our team?"

"Uh, I think one other guy—his name is Mark."

Just then three cars pulled up to the curb and out came four guys, Stevo and Nick, Tom and Mark.

Each one had a better excuse than the other for coming late. One's alarm clock broke, another said he went to sleep at 11:30am having been up all night partying, a third got bombed and woke up with a terrible headache, and the fourth said he worked all night. Lester and long-haired Lou showed up a few minutes later so that made eight guys. We went through the motions again this time with a little more intensity but not enough to show anyone really cared. I thought to myself "I can't believe this is the 'other' league."

Tom was leaning up against the fence in center because he wasn't sober enough to stand on his own two feet. Maybe Amy had something to do with it. Easy fly balls would fall in and out of his glove and he made no attempts to run after a ball. I couldn't imagine how we would win with guys like this on the team. But to be fair, maybe he had an off night. Maybe he doesn't get sloshed every Saturday night. Little did I know that he wanted to play shortstop very badly.

With only about half the team on the field it was tough to sense who was going to play which position. We rotated on the field as we each took our turns at bat—our defense had a lot to be desired. And our hitting could not be gauged properly because of the ridiculous right-field situation, and the lack of a decent softball to hit. We had one ball—and we had to practically knock the cover off of it in order to get it by the outfielders who were playing shallow. The selection of bats was also poor—two of them—one felt like forty-eight ounces (very heavy) and the other was shorter than my nineteen month old son. The only thing that resembled a game was when Lester led part of the practice by yelling out a situation and then hit the ball to see how the defense would react. For example: "Man on third one out". He then hits a fly ball to left field. The throw came into third base. "Why didn't you fire the ball home?" Lester fumed. "Because there's no friggin' catcher behind you!" answered Mark. We got the hang of it by the twentieth try. It taught us that we were in trouble executing the basics.

After the practice I gave Lenny the money and pictures. The team picture didn't look rosy but I figured it could only get better from now on. So I thought.

CHAPTER THREE

OPENING DAY

After the last practice I had an empty feeling inside of me. Having already been stripped of my initial enthusiasm and eagerness, it didn't look as if things were going to change a lot by next Sunday's opener. Nonetheless, I was very much looking forward to Sunday at 6pm. I specifically remember asking Lenny if he was sure about the starting time because the clocks were not scheduled to be changed to daylight savings time until the week after. He said definitely yes—a 6pm start. Who was I to argue?

Sunday arrived. I couldn't eat a whole day. Our uniforms hadn't arrived at our last practice so I just donned black sweatpants, a white tee shirt, and a warm-up jacket. I drove over to Avenue X and Bedford Avenue to be on time for warm-ups but instead I see a game in progress. It couldn't be! I tried to ascertain the team from the uniforms - ours was black with white and gray trim plus WARRIORS printed across the front. I quickly parked the car and walked up to the field from behind home plate. I looked toward the dugout and saw our team all there—except for me.

"The game started?" I intoned incredulously.

"Yeah, we're in the second inning."

"But Len said the game starts at 6!"

The game started at five. I ran over to Lou and asked him for my uniform. He opened a box and pulled out a #18 jersey. It was a bit chilly as I peeled off my jacket. I quickly pulled the shirt over my head trying to look as inconspicuous as possible. I felt embarrassed enough coming "late", and now it seemed as if I was putting on the uniform in full view of both teams. At that moment I noticed a "10" looking right at me. "That must be Amy" I murmured under my breath.

I looked out toward the field. Our team was already in trouble. I didn't recognize all the guys out there since not all showed up at one time at practices. I was also furious at Lenny because had I come on time I would have started at shortstop. Instead Tom was there. Remember? He's the one who couldn't stand up straight at the first practice.

The score was already 5-0 in the other team's favor. Our pitcher, Roger, was having trouble getting the ball over the plate. When he finally did, the ball was hit to shortstop—actually twice in a row. And both times Tom booted the ball. I felt bad for the team and still steaming I wasn't out there. We finally got them out. Dejected, the team came into the dugout. One or two acknowledged my presence. Lenny wasn't one of them.

In all fairness to Lenny, his mind was scattered in so many places, he couldn't focus in on anyone or on anything. I guess that was part of the problem. To be an effective manager, one has got to have the overview and at the same time be able to maneuver effectively while focusing on the details. This is a hard enough task to perform under normal circumstances. Needless to say, these were not normal circumstances. Mark was bitching away at not starting the game. He accused Lenny of not knowing what he is doing. Even if he was right, saying it in full earshot of all was horrible. Each time an error was committed, everyone would get on the player and let him know what a "good job" he was doing for the team. Then the players would turn on Lenny for not having the foresight to place people in their proper positions. As the game got more and more out of hand, more pressure came from the bench warmers to get some playing time. Mark summed it up nicely: "I didn't pay seventy dollars to watch you guys make errors."

The whole situation got so bad it was downright pathetic. Trailing 13-1 in the third inning, twelve errors having been committed, a hoard of biting, cutting, malicious, accusatory remarks were aimed toward each others' hitting and fielding performances. Webster's Collegiate Dictionary defines a team as a group of persons associated together in work or activity. Teamwork is that which is done by a number of associates each doing a part, but all subordinating personal prominence to the efficiency of the whole. The Warriors were far from this ideal.

I did get a chance to enter the game in the fourth inning. Standing at shortstop somehow I felt uncomfortable. I don't know what came over me but it was a feeling I hadn't experienced in a very long time. Maybe I felt inadequate because I was surrounded by mediocrity. Maybe it was the fact that our opponent that day, the boys from Canarsie, was a team in every sense of the word. They hit well, fielded well, and displayed a relaxed, yet competitive attitude throughout the game. They clapped, cheered, and jokingly ribbed any teammate who couldn't get on base against us. They were a unit. It only highlighted our own team's sorrowful state.

Already leading by a mile, Canarsie continued to pound the ball. No. 21, a guy with the name Nova printed above the number on his back, stepped to the plate and proceeded to drill the first pitch off the right field fence for a triple.

"Way to go Nove!"

"Come on Nove, you coulda made it home on that", came a sarcastic jeer from their bench.

The next batter lined a double to left which was followed by a walk. A groundout to first advanced the runners to second and third with one out. Then a pop out to short center, runners holding. The ball hadn't come near me yet and I didn't even have a chance to touch the ball save for one practice throw. A cold wind blew slightly; I was practically stiff.

The next pitch was bounced sharply in the hole at short. I took one short step to my right and stuck out my backhand to snare the ball. Instead, the ball hit the tip of my glove and continued on its way to left field. E-6.

It was a ball I should have handled. I knew that. But, of course, it was reinforced by some members of the team—especially the ones who were making errors all game long and who were now sitting on the bench.

I was embarrassed and angry. Embarrassed in front of all who saw the play because they probably figured I was an error-maker just like the others. And angry because I knew that I wouldn't be playing shortstop after today.

I felt cheated because I didn't get another chance that inning. One ball did come close, but it went out into left-center just out of my reach. I still heard the tisks and tasks about my not reaching it.

Some of the guys were saying how embarrassed they were, especially in front of their friends and girlfriends who came to the game. It didn't seem like Tom cared much about what Amy thought. I had recently heard that the last girl Tom was seeing got pregnant from him. He forced her to undergo an abortion. What began as a sweet relationship ended in bitter resentment. He treated her like dirt and paid her off to keep quiet about the whole thing and threatened her if she didn't. I saw Amy headed in the same direction.

In our half of the inning, the Canarsie captain decided to change pitchers. Their number two pitcher started the game and he pitched well, but probably looked better than he was because we weren't hitting. I was the scheduled lead-off batter. When I saw their number 1 pitcher wearing #16 warm up on the mound, I said to myself "why me?" He was considered to be the fastest pitcher in the league. Why they brought him in at this point in the game is something I never figured out. The umpire informed us that if we didn't score at least five runs in this inning, he would have to call the game by virtue of the mercy rule. That sure pumped us up.

I studied his motion and prayed I would somehow just get a piece of the ball. I stepped up to the plate and waited. The first pitch was a bullet that cut the plate right in half for strike one. The next pitch started out high and inside and wound up high and outside. I had never seen movement like that before by a softball. He then threw me a fastball, but again it was outside. Good, maybe he'll walk me. His teammates encouraged him to pitch to me—in other words, let me hit it. He threw a change-up which completely screwed up the timing of my swing. I fouled the ball back off the screen behind me. I could tell #16 was toying with me. Up came his arms to a point and then down before hurling. I was looking to hit it up the middle for a single. Instead, since I couldn't control my bat speed, I pulled a sharp grounder toward second base. When I first hit it, I thought it would go into right-center field. But the second-baseman took two steps to his right and made the play. One out. Disappointed, I went back to the dugout, but with rejuvenated interest as if I had somehow just won the battle. It was quite an accomplishment not to strike out against this guy. While I didn't receive any pats on the back for my performance, I didn't get any jeers either. He then proceeded to mow down the next two batters with relative ease.

The result was a call by the umpire to stop the game in the fifth inning due to the mercy rule; the score was 17-1. I overheard one of the umpires saying to the other: "This team has no business being in this league." He was right. I couldn't help but think about the types of errors that were made and the number of walks given up. It was no different than the Sunday morning choose-up game—only there, at least the guys had the ability to laugh at themselves—no threats, no accusations, no hard feelings.

The traditional line-up for handshakes after the game was over was a nice gesture and was perhaps one of the few redeeming features of the league. The team we played was last year's champs and they certainly proved it on the field.

We gathered in our dugout for the post-mortem. The comments were all quite revealing:

"Boy do we need practice."

"We could've been in the game if we didn't make stupid errors."

"It looks like we are going to switch a few people around in the field".

"If Lenny knew what he was doing out there we may have had a chance."

There were other directed spears that hit the Lenny target. I felt bad for him—especially since some of these were made in the presence of his father. Stevo, though, stepped in and said the loss was a team effort. He offered to help Lenny out in managing and said he would take on a share of the responsibility in running the team. Since mid-week practices seemed almost impossible to schedule, it was suggested to go to a batting range to beef up on the hitting. The fielding would improve by altering the positions.

Nobody walked away pleased at anything that transpired during that brief meeting. But the feeling was that we had to play better just to survive within our own ranks. Today I arrived at the field at 5:15pm and returned home at 6:30pm. In practically no time, so much took place—and a lot was to be learned.

At 8:30pm Gerald called. He asked me how it went.

"We got killed. We had two hits the whole game. It was called after five innings."

"What was the score?"

"If I must tell you—17-1."

"Oh that's OK. We lost 1-0."

"You're kidding." I smiled to myself.

"No. We were one-hit."

"How ironic. But at least your game was exciting."

"Exciting? It was the most boring game I've played in."

"Our loss, though, was devastating," I said. "Every time someone made an error, nasty comments were flying. The attitude of these kids, no, these babies, really bother me. And guess what else? I didn't start at short. You know why? Because I was told the game starts at 6pm. So I show up at 5:15 and the game is already in the second inning!"

"Well, look at it this way. There are four other teams with the same record as ours."

We both cracked up.

CHAPTER FOUR

RIGHT FIELD OR BUST

During the week I gave considerable thought to that first game. As the elder statesman on the team I began to think that maybe I should take some leadership and knock some sense into these kids. The average age on our team was twenty—the league average was thirty.

I decided to take the indirect approach. I called Lenny on Wednesday night and told him how disgusted I was at the attitudes of the players, especially those who bad-mouthed him.

"Where did you pick up these guys from?" I asked.

"On the whole", Lenny told me, "they're decent ballplayers, but they're just very immature and it showed itself in the game."

"Those guys have got to be told to cut the crap because we can't go on as a team like this."

"You're right. But you know how it is—everybody wants to play. Somebody is gonna be unhappy."

"Not if you lay down some rules right from the outset. Those who don't like it can leave. Tell everyone that a system of rotation will be in place starting next game so that everyone gets equal playing time—even if it means that our best player sits for three innings. We all paid money to be in the league, so everybody's got to play. Once that is understood, there will be less noise. Now for the hard part. Either you or Stevo must tell the crew that you are the team captain. Then get five or six guys who will stand by your word and who will jump in the middle of a potential flare-up and give hell to anyone who criticizes or embarrasses you or anyone else. Count me in as one. Only then could we concentrate on playing the game right, instead of wondering how not to make the next mistake."

"Thanks. What you're saying makes a lot of sense. Stevo is coming over in about fifteen minutes and I'll tell him what you said. He basically thinks that the guys acted like a bunch of three-year olds, and even told off Nick and Curt after the game on Sunday."

"I'm glad to hear that."

"I think things will get better."

"Well, they could hardly get worse."

"I mean, we're going to re-arrange positions. Roger walked too many guys. We're going to try him at shortstop. He's a really good athlete. Lester will pitch. We haven't figured out the other spots."

"Can Roger handle shortstop?" I was hoping he would answer with some doubt. My insides were screaming 'what about me?'

"Yeah, he's played it before. Tom was awful at short last week and I know you didn't have a chance to prove yourself. If Roger doesn't work out, you'll get a shot."

Concealing my true thoughts I just said "Sounds good. I understand. I could play the outfield if that is where I will best help the team." After I said that I wished I hadn't opened my mouth so wide.

"There's my bell. It's probably Stevo. I'll see ya Sunday."

"What time?" I asked.

"Six o'clock's the game. Come at 4:30 for some extra practice."

"Are you sure?"

"Yeah, last week was at five. We're changing the clocks back an hour this Saturday night so we play at six. The days are getting' longer, ya know."

"Lenny, the clocks are moved forward in the spring. Ya know, spring forward, fall back".

"Are you sure?"

"As sure as I remember you telling me that last week's game was to start at six."

"I said that?"

"Yeah, that's why I showed up in the third inning."

"Hey, I'm really sorry. I thought I called everyone during the week telling them it was at five".

"Well, nobody called me. By the way, had I come on time, would I have started at short?"

No response. The silence was deafening. I prompted for an answer.

"I know I'm putting you on the spot, but you can be honest with me. I can handle it."

"Tom wanted to play short real bad. I was thinking of starting either one of you at short and you'd split the game."

"He put a lot of pressure on you, didn't he?"

"In a manner of speaking, yes."

What could I say? It was no use. I was trying to force myself up a creek against the current with no paddle.

It was 4:30pm on Sunday April 28, 1985. The pre-game warm-up was delayed—it was pouring. I pulled up to the field at the corner of Albany Avenue and Glenwood Road. Even though it was daytime, the sky was dark. I stayed in the car listening to the Met game on the radio. They were tied in the ninth inning against the Pirates.

A game was in progress despite the rain. The downpour was heavy but both teams remained on the field. I thought these guys were either really dedicated to the game, hadn't showered in a long time, or were just plain crazy. All were distinct possibilities.

Peering through my wet window I saw a man get on base with a single. The ball was waterlogged and slowed down considerably by the time it reached the outfielder. The runner sloshed his way to first and I was able to see water stomped out the sides of his sneakers. Those socks must have felt like wet towels.

An hour passed and the rain let up a bit. The sky was getting lighter and the chances for playing today started to look better. The Mets were now in the fourteenth inning still tied. The previous game's wet players had already left the field and some of the Warriors ventured out in the drizzle and onto the puddle-laden infield. I didn't want to get out of the car because I didn't want to talk to anyone. Besides, I was glued to the Met game.

The confines of my Dodge Aries K represented a temporary refuge from the harsh reality of the concrete and stone. But it wasn't to be for long. As the rainclouds drew further apart, more of our guys appeared on the field. It was time to join them.

It was strange going out to the field and not knowing what position to go to. We were just throwing the ball around getting ready for batting practice. I hung out in the dugout for a while but seeing that Lenny made no attempt to tell me where to play, I trotted out to center field since nobody was there yet. I shagged some flies, including some that had wings, and then Curt showed up.

"Hey, why don't I move to right?" I said.

Looks like I dug myself into a hole at right.

At first I couldn't get used to it. The angle of the ball coming off the bat was very tough to adjust to. But I thought that this was only practice—surely I wouldn't be playing out here in the game.

Not many balls were hit my way during practice. All of our batters were right-handed, and with the lob pitching, everyone was cracking the ball to left and center. There was, however, one ball hit towards me. On a late inside-out swing the ball was popped up about twenty feet past first base and up the right-field line. I was in right-center at the time. I figured since I hadn't touched the ball yet, perhaps it was time to go after it. I ran as hard as I could as I watched the ball drop faster and faster. My hat flew off and my glasses were sliding down my nose. I felt a cramp in my right thigh.

My sneakers were not gripping the wet pavement all that well. I then extended my glove just enough for the ball to fall into it while my inertia took me into the fence. Good thing it was there—it probably prevented a bad spill.

"All right! Nice catch!"

"Beauty".

"Way to hustle out there."

I believe that clinched the right-field spot for me.

We each took a turn at bat and then rested in the dugout until game time. We also got a pep talk from Lenny.

"Listen guys, we looked pretty good out there in practice. Last week we didn't know who should play where and we got clobbered. We weren't prepared for the game, but we should do much better today. The team we're playing is not overpowering and we should be able to do well out there. If we just play smart and throw to the right base and keep a good attitude, we'll be okay. If someone makes an error, it's okay. We do the best we can. If we support each other out there instead of what happened last week, we'll be able to have more concentration for the game. Part of last week was my fault and I'm sorry for that. I'm gonna try to get everyone in the game. So here's the starting lineup and batting order:

29 Curt	CF
20 Tom	LF
14 Roger	SS
17 Jason	1B
15 Lester	P
12 Lenny	2B
9 Lou	SCF
13 Stevo	C
18 Bernie	RF
33 Nick	3B

I actually talked my way into playing right-field. From shortstop no less. I felt it was a step down but at least I was in the starting lineup.

Let me now introduce you to the rest of our cast of characters:

Tom stood about 5'7" and looked like Harpo Marx, although his sense of humor would be more appropriately compared to the number zero. He didn't impress me from the moment I met him. He was also very jealous. I would overhear him trying to undercut me by saying I couldn't handle shortstop, and that he is better suited for it. He would constantly be telling the team captain not to let me play short. He would never extend the courtesy to let me or anyone else play the position he wanted. During practices, I would do well at shortstop and he couldn't stand it. He would never acknowledge a nice play. The others did. He saw me as a threat and sought to take me down even if he takes himself and the team down in the process. He never greeted me, never initiated a hello, nor answered a greeting when approached. Out of all the guys on the team, he, by far, earned the award for having the worst personality on the team. Why Amy goes out with him is beyond me. I couldn't figure out what was attracting her to this creep. Moreover, watching Stevo making advances to impress her with his foul antics was also downright nauseating. Tom and Stevo were good friends, but I had a sense that wasn't going to last too long.

Roger was our resident high school jock. Unassuming and reserved, he let his bat and glove do all the talking for him. He was, in my opinion, our best all-around player. He was sound in the basics, fielded shortstop very well and hit the ball each time he came to bat. He never complained nor criticized anyone for making an error. Believe it or not, I was happy about him playing shortstop. I couldn't say that for anyone else on the team. I wish we had ten more like him.

Our first-baseman was our number four hitter but deserved to bat twelfth. Jason was very tall and powerfully built. The number 17 on his jersey approximated his age but he would have spurts of acting in a more mature manner in certain situations. For example, he would shout encouraging words and clap with enthusiasm as a teammate would step to the plate. He would occasionally offer words of solace after an out and then quickly become positive about the next hitter. He was, nevertheless, our biggest disappointment at the plate. He was to provide run production, power, and the big threat. Unfortunately, he couldn't hit his way out of a wet paper bag. He tried to hit the ball over the fence each time he batted. After striking out and popping up consistently over the first few games, he decided he was over-swinging and then tried to half-swing with the hope of blooping the ball over an infielder. In order to do this right, one would need very good bat control. Needless to say, Jason didn't have it. Maybe the reason he was so positive about the others was because he was in no position to criticize anybody else. If that was so, at least he recognized it.

Lester was assigned to the mound in game two. He didn't pitch all that badly, but he was constantly in trouble walking batters. He seemed intent on winning and was generally concerned with the way the team was run. He would not be afraid to let you know if you made a defensive error (like missing the cut-off on a throw from the outfield). He would often get emotional about an error or an out, but in his own way, he showed that he cared.

Lou made a good impression on me from the start. Short and plump with an even-tempered disposition, Lou showed up at the first practice sporting long hair, a Fu Manchu mustache, and a beer belly. He was pleasant to talk to and brought his jolly attitude with him. Despite his build, he fielded well and could hit—at one point he became our most consistent hitter. Lou did shock us, however, before one game. He showed up clean-shaven with a 1958 crew cut. It made this pizza shop owner look even fatter. But it didn't affect his hitting. He would later become the manager of the team.

We had three other guys on the team bringing the total to thirteen. Andy, #11, an import from Jersey, was a very well-built athlete. He didn't say much, but answered when he was spoken to. He would play the outfield and had some pop to his bat. We often sat next to each other on the bench philosophizing on the game, bemoaning Amy's mismatch with Tom, and wondering what the heck he was doing wasting his time playing for this team. He had trouble finding the fields we were scheduled to play on. I felt for him—he was a nice guy. Wouldn't it be nice, I thought, if he could win Amy over. During the first couple of weeks, he only managed to fantasize about her, but didn't have the guts to approach her. He was much better-looking than Tom, and had some class.

Roland, #22, was to have been my original competition for the shortstop job, but he ended up in the outfield like me. His season was curtailed, however, as he slipped and fell hard on his knee going for a long outfield drive. He was told by his doctor not to play on the torn ligaments, so he came down to the remaining games as a coach. I never said he was bright.

Big Mark, #77, always seemed as if he had a big microphone in front of his mouth. He became louder and more boisterous as each practice and game went by. Constantly voicing his displeasure at the way the team was run, it came mostly out of frustration that he wasn't a starter. He waddled as he walked, carrying a big frame and pot belly. His bitching about who should play where, and where he should play got on my nerves. He was a chronic whiner and constantly embarrassed Lenny in front of others by uttering comments such as:

"You suck as a manager. You don't know what the %#$& you are doing."

"Who the hell do you think you are telling me where to play? I don't want to play short-center even in practice."

"On the team I was on last year, we were organized and I played third base. I could play it as good as anyone here. Why are you playing second base? I think you suck at second. Why don't you sit yourself down and let me play second?"

Nice guy. The only good thing about his berating style was that nobody else on the team sided with him. He was recognized as a cry-baby loud mouth and it served him justice that he wasn't given a starting assignment.

After the pep talk the atmosphere in the dugout seemed much more spirited. The sky, though, remained dark and overcast; the humidity was in the high 90's. Puddles of water pervaded the concrete outfield—all for the making of a treacherous evening. One of the two umpires was late as it was already past game time. I was beginning to wonder whether he'd arrive safely as five police cars were cruising the area. To their credit, they didn't stop to watch the game.

So the game started with one umpire. The ground rules were a bit different in each of the four fields we used. This park had a short right-field fence with tree branches hanging over the top of the twenty-one foot high fence. The braches were majestic looking, each with a full set of leaves emanating from its stem. An occasional wind would send down a couple of drops of rain onto the ground thereby increasing the fluid content of each puddle in which it landed.

Center-field was the deepest part of the park and left-field was further from home plate than right-field. Any ball hit over the right-field fence was an automatic single. The further the ball traveled toward the poles in right-center, it was either a double or homerun. It looked easy to pop the ball over the fence, but that kind of thinking usually resulted in pop ups to the infield. Our team was a master thinker in this regard.

We faced a left-handed pitcher who had a rather decent fastball. Nothing tricky, though. He should have been very hittable. But we were thinking too much and alas they had an easy time catching lazy fly balls. Lester pitched well for us but he was giving out too many free passes. It would eventually hurt us.

The second umpire finally showed up between the second and third inning. He excused himself for being late and blamed it on the Mass Transit Authority. The game was scoreless until the bottom of the fourth inning. Their first two batters walked. A pop up to the infield and a force at second accounted for two outs—runners were now on first and third. It looked as if we were going to get out of the inning with no runs scored. But the next pitch was bounced to third where the ball was handled by Nick. Unfortunately as he backed up to snare the bouncer, he lost his footing on the wet pavement, fell on his behind, and couldn't get up in time to complete the play. The score stood at 1-0, but as we trotted off the field after the third out, we were confident that we would get that run back and more.

I came up to bat for the second time in the fifth inning after having flied out to center already. Batting right-handed after taking batting practice left-handed felt a bit uncomfortable, but I did manage to hit the ball hard in my first at-bat. I was trying to find a hole to smack it through. I saw a gap in right-center. I waited for my pitch, a high outside fastball. I connected solidly and it sailed toward the gap in right-center. But out of nowhere the right-fielder cut across the wet pavement with reckless abandon and ran the ball down. I was now 0 for 2.

The sixth inning was uneventful—just as the rest of the game was. Our team could have played without me standing in right-field—not one ball came even close. We started getting nervous as the top of the seventh and final inning arrived. We hadn't mounted any serious threats during the entire game. While we were pleased to have played well defensively, our hitting remained dormant. I was the fourth batter scheduled up in the inning. Our morale was a bit shot, but the dugout clung to whatever hope there was left. Each batter got more than usual encouragement, which was nice for a change. I did, though, overhear someone say "if we can't score even one run, then we really suck."

Our first two batters grounded out and flied out respectively. As I stepped onto the on-deck circle, I was thinking how I always hated being the last out. My struggle to root for Lou to get on base was slowly losing to my fear of being the potential last out of the game. Teammates always seem to remember who made the last out. You could go 3 for 3, but if you make the last out of the game, that's what they will remember.

As fate would have it, Lou walked. Our last hope now rested on my shoulders. I became the focus of attention. There must have been some concession among some of the players as I stepped to the plate. I tried to block that out of my mind. I looked at the defense and decided to go up the middle. I drew the count to 2 and 0. The next pitch was likely to be right down the middle, but we needed base runners, so I took a pitch. "Strike one." The pitcher could not afford to walk me. Everyone on the field knew it. I could not afford to make the last out—only I knew that. I gazed in at the mound, my eyes affixed on the left hand of the pitcher. As his arm came back I cocked my bat. The pitch was right down the middle of the plate. I swung and the ball rocketed off my bat. The ball reached the outfield so fast I hardly had a chance to drop the bat. Amy gave a shrill. I watched the ball sail towards the deepest part of the park. But it wasn't to be. The center-fielder nonchalantly took a few steps back and reached up to grab it for the final out.

I couldn't look anybody in the eye as I got back to the dugout nor would anybody say anything to me. I guess that was good in comparison to last week's game.

The team stuck around for the post-game recap. We all agreed we played well defensively but were very down on our non-hitting. We hit some balls hard but right at somebody. Maybe it was the fortunate positioning of the opponents. Maybe the pitcher was better than he seemed. Maybe it was fate. Maybe we just suck.

The Mets wound up pounding through an eighteen inning game—at least they found a way to win.

Gerald called me later in the evening. He reported that his team beat the team that mauled us last week. Down 2-1 in the last inning, fireballer #16 went wild and walked five straight batters. He then reminded me of our upcoming double-header in three weeks. I shuddered at the thought.

CHAPTER FIVE

SWEATING IT OUT

When I originally convinced myself that this league would be worth a try, I rationalized that in terms of a time commitment it would not be any different than playing first thing in the morning. As a matter of fact, I thought a 6pm start would be better; I could sleep late, enjoy the whole day, and cap it off with a game in the evening.

I was wrong. First of all, I couldn't sleep late; my kids would wake me at 6:15am. Not having a game to look forward to in the morning, made me unhappy about being up that early on a Sunday morning. It was almost sacrilegious. Secondly, it was hard to enjoy the whole day knowing I had to be mentally and physically prepared for the game. "Don't run to the corner or you'll pull a muscle"; "don't buy ice cream, you may get an upset stomach"; "don't drive out to New

Jersey to visit friends, you may not make it back in time". I was truly under the spell of the game. It determined my schedule, my thought patterns, and my activities. I was no longer in control.

The first sign of this revelation was that I was losing weight. I didn't have to be a genius to figure out that it was attributed to my not eating a whole day. My body couldn't take food in for hours before a game. I would manage to eat a light breakfast, but beyond that, until I would wind down from the game late at night, I couldn't even look at food.

The second sign was my impatience with the rest of the events of the day. I would rush my wife out of shopping centers, cut short her phone conversations with friends, and not spend enough time in the park with my kids. My attention span and temper grew very short; I became a general pain in the butt to everyone and to myself.

It took me about two weeks to realize the effect I was having on my family. Bits of information that would be passed along to me were going in one ear and out the other. I was being downright selfish. I couldn't continue along this path, so I began rethinking my priorities vis a vis this new league.

Having a record of 0 and 2 wasn't the end of the world. After all, many good teams have lousy starts and come back to have great seasons. Our two losses were at opposite ends of the spectrum—we got clobbered and eked out. Now all we had to do was lose some in the middle range to make our experience complete.

It is interesting how people cope with losing. Some will blame the loss on the fact that the winner cheated. Others will want to forget what happened and will then proceed to drink themselves to sleep. Some take it out on their family and yet others will not care. The most gracious loser, however, is the one who can accept the loss with a healthy perspective.

Of course, depending on the way one loses could influence one's subsequent reaction. Getting pounded 17-1 is not a good feeling, but hey, give credit to the other team's hitters. If it was the result of twelve errors, then a different set of responses would be likely.

In this context I couldn't help to think about the way George Steinbrenner ran the Yankees. He hated to lose. Anything less than a championship season for him was a big disappointment to say the least. He would have little patience for mediocrity and fired his team's managers often. He was not a believer in nice guys don't always finish last.

I wonder whether all of the aggravation, embarrassment, hurt and humiliation inflicted on his managers and ballplayers were washed away by winning a world series. It isn't always the bottom line that counts—how you get there is sometimes just as important and may even have longer-lasting effects on the players involved.

Years ago I worked in a New Jersey hospital and joined their league softball team.

It was co-ed and the idea was to get out and have a good time; winning was not the primary objective. There was, however, an opportunity to play for the win in a highly touted game between staff and the administration. As a young member of the administration, I came with an attitude to play to win—I didn't want to give the staff a chance to win and have it rubbed into us as I thought they would. I planned on fielding a team that was as solid as possible at every position. As the game went along we had a narrow lead, but the chief administrator, Tom Doolan, wanted to substitute some of the starting players with less talented ones. While I wasn't one of those being substituted, I still questioned the move. His response is one that I'll always remember. He told me:

"The important thing about this game is that everybody who came down should play—even if it is for only one inning because ten years from now nobody is going to remember the score as much as whether they played or not".

He was absolutely right. Years later I didn't remember many details, but I do remember that I played and had a good time. By the way, we ended up clobbering them 24-8.

I missed yesterday's practice—on purpose. Not because I didn't think I needed it, but because it was the Sabbath. I never told anyone on the team that I was an observant Jew. It was clear to me from the outset that this bit of information was not necessary to mention. I just wanted to blend into the background of the team. I had some very good reasons for doing this. Growing up in the Flatlands section of Brooklyn, a predominantly Jewish neighborhood, many young boys frequented the streets adorning skullcaps without fear of vindictive remarks or physical assault. There were, however, occasions when riding the city bus to and from school or walking down certain streets resulted in both.

So I wanted to enter the league without any undue pressure. Moreover, I wanted to be judged as a ballplayer with no biases attached.

Game 3 of the season was against a team who were similar in age and make-up to ours. They looked beatable as we watched them taking batting practice. Unfortunately, to them we probably looked equally pulverizable.

While preparing for the game I thought about how being a switch hitter has its advantages. For as long as I can remember, I wanted to be able to do it well. Over the years I developed into a more consistent left-handed hitter simply because I faced more right-handed pitching. In game 2 I batted exclusively lefty in practice assuming a right-handed pitcher would start for the opposition. Nobody was warming up on the sidelines and the other team didn't want to volunteer the info that a lefty was pitching. So I went 0 for 3 in that game. For this game, I took no chances. I took ten swings—five righty and five lefty. Seven of the ten were pop-ups to the infield. The other three were weak grounders. You could say I wasn't impressive at the plate. This didn't discourage me, though, because there wasn't always a positive correlation between pre-game and game performance. The conditions are different; the psyche is not the same. The only good indicator of batting practice is that it could tip you off on whether you feel comfortable at the plate or not and how your timing measures up. Adjustments are made at this point—where the ball goes is not necessarily important. At least that's what I thought.

In the first inning of the game we were already behind. A couple of hits, an error and a missed cut-off throw by Curt produced two quick runs.

I came to bat in the second inning with two outs and a runner on third. I felt that I could hit this pitcher—he had good control and was not overpowering. I tried to block out my terrible hitting performance during batting practice. The first pitch was down the middle of the plate. I'd never see a fat pitch like that again. The next pitch was high. I had an opportunity to get our team on the board early in the game. It would be an important boost for the team and for me personally. Surprisingly, the next pitch came right down the middle. I swung hard and level and the ball screamed out into right-center field for a single and an RBI.

As I took the turn around first, I watched the right-fielder get the throw back into the infield. My teammates, all on their feet, were awakened at the crack of the bat.

"Awright, way to go!"

"Solid."

"Yeah, clutch hit, man."

The first hit of the season was a sweet one. It accounted for a run, it aroused the team and it built up my confidence. I was now convinced that I could hit in this league. It's quite amazing what a difference a hit makes. Already I was thinking "hey, this league isn't so bad after all." The unpleasantness of the last few weeks started to dissipate. There was actually hope for this team and this season.

Well, perhaps my feelings in the moment got the better of me. We didn't score any more that inning or for the rest of the game. It remained 2-1 until the last inning when they scored a run on a walk and two hits—no errors this time. The final was 3-1. Nobody needed an accountant to tally the runs produced by our invisible offense over the first three games—two. Pitiful. But at least the last two games were tight defensive battles in which we played rather well. Our offense lacked just one important ingredient—hitting. You could play defense all day, but unlike other sports, the defensive team in baseball cannot score. While I stood as our hitting "star" in this game, it was inappropriate to feel too good about it. Sure it gave me a shot in the arm, but it's hard to enjoy individual success when the rest of the team is so down.

I didn't hear from Gerald that evening—his team must have lost too.

CHAPTER SIX

PAST GLORY, PRESENT

DRUDGERY

My father, of blessed memory, was an avid baseball fan. He always used to tell me that on any given day, any team can beat another. But as a kid, I was the ultimate pessimist. When we faced a little league team that was undefeated, I would say something like "oh, we can't beat them—they've got the best pitcher in the league and two guys who could hit the ball over the fence." But my father was the eternal optimist. Even if he didn't think we could win, he'd always *say* we could. To a 10-year old, that kind of encouragement meant a lot. I could then remain hopeful that our team, sponsored that year by Scott's Bootery, could actually beat Tina's Cake Fair.

One of the first experiences I had in this regard was the 1969 All-Star competition between an array of little leagues in Brooklyn. Amity Little League had never before won a game in all-star competition, where a team who loses just one ballgame is automatically disqualified from advancing to the next round. We knew we had a good team and felt that we could win despite having a won-loss record of 1-3 in the four exhibition games we played.

I was the starting left-fielder. I actually played second-base during the season but was placed in the outfield because I had a strong arm. At the age of twelve, it was my first selection to the all-star team. We were clad in special uniforms and given individual attention during each practice session. We learned the fine art of stealing a base, sliding, how to get up quickly after a slide in case the ball goes astray, how to bunt, and how to utilize the cut-off man in varying situations. I learned more about the fundamentals of baseball in those few weeks than I did the entire six years playing in the league. It was a terrific feeling; we were made to feel like all-stars by our coaching staff. We loved it and each player gave one hundred and ten percent at all times.

All of the games were played at a neutral park, Kings Bay Field—a very well-kept diamond designed specifically for little league baseball. It actually looked like a miniature major league ballpark. There were real dugouts, an electric scoreboard and American flag beyond the center-field fence, advertisements along the perimeter of the outfield walls, chalk lines along the bases and in the batter's box, an elevated mound with a resin bag, grandstands, a concession, and best of all, a press box behind home plate. We used to get a real kick out of being individually introduced by the public address (P.A.) announcer as each team took their pre-game place along the third and first-base lines. Then off came the caps while a tape of the Star Spangled Banner played. The P.A. system made the whole all-star experience a memorable one. It was exhilarating to be announced before each at-bat in front of a large crowd.

Our first game was against Greenpoint. There was a lot of pressure to finally win one since Amity had always been eliminated in the first round. We watched Greenpoint take batting practice and weren't impressed until a 6'2" 13-year old took his swings. He was popping the ball over the deepest part of center-field with ease. If we could contain him, we would have a good chance. Our pitcher, Scott, not only contained him, but pitched a no-hitter. He walked quite a few, but we shut them out 3-0. Oh, the jubilation! Amity finally broke its losing streak. We all mobbed Scott before the traditional handshaking ceremony between the two teams.

Our next opponent was West Brighton. We had defeated this team in our only victory in exhibition play, so naturally, we felt confident. I remember one of my at-bats as if it took place just yesterday. Their pitcher was a left-hander with a very deliberate motion. I stepped up to the plate having been given the "take" sign from our third base coach. It was a fastball right on the outside corner—but to my amazement, the umpire called it a "ball". I crowded the plate and took the next three pitches all in the exact same spot. They were all called balls. The umpire must have had a very small strike zone. I dropped the bat and hustled to first-base lest the umpire decided to change his mind. I ended up walking three times. Steve, our pitcher, also pitched a no-hitter, but West Brighton scored three runs on walks and a couple of errors; we prevailed, though, 5-3.

The third game will be forever implanted in my mind as the most exciting game I've ever played. It was the semi-final game for the all-star championship. If we win, we go to the finals. Scheduled to face us was North Highway—our nemesis in exhibition—we lost twice to them. Immediately following our win over West Brighton, our team was told who our next opponent would be. Our coaches thought that they would tell us while we were on a high from two straight wins. But the highs turned to "oh no's" very quickly. Our two losses to them were convincing ones. They seemed to do everything well. What impressed me most was their hustle. On a walk they would run to first base.

We had a couple of days to prepare for the game. During practices our confidence was restored, and the prospect of losing to them disappeared.

The game proceeded as we hoped it wouldn't. They led 5-2 going into the last inning. We managed to load the bases with one out and I stepped up to the plate.

At this point, North Highway made a pitching change bringing in their right-fielder to the mound. This left-hander looked like a bowling ball but pitched effectively against us in exhibition. I had to turn around to bat right-handed.

Thus far in the series, I had one hit in seven official at-bats plus four walks. My one hit came batting lefty. Since I was the number two hitter in the lineup, it was important for me not to hit into any kind of double play. Then again, it's important for anyone in that situation not to hit into a double play.

The first pitch was right down the middle for a strike. The next pitch was a fastball on the outside half of the plate which I lined foul down the right-field line. A walk was a virtual impossibility; I had to protect myself with a two-strike count.

The runners took short leads from each base. There was a lot of noise from the crowd and from the dugouts, but the only thing I heard was my heart pumping faster and faster.

The pitcher went into his windup and down came the arm with another fastball about to slice the middle of the plate. I swung and met the ball with the meat of the bat. It whistled past the pitcher on the ground toward the second base bag. The second-baseman dove for the ball but came up empty. The ball continued into center-field. One run scored to make it 5-3. The runner from second also tried to score, but the center-fielder gunned him down at the plate. On the play, I continued on to second base with the runner ahead of me advancing to third.

Now there were two outs and our number three hitter Steven Berkowitz at bat. The first pitch was lined deep to left-field, going, going, gone—foul! The ball missed being fair by less than a foot. Our hearts fell into our stomachs.

Wasting no time, Steve swung at the very next pitch and bounced one deep in the hole at shortstop. I held my position and watched the runner from third head for home. The shortstop backhanded the ball and to my surprise tried to throw Steve out at first base. As soon as he threw it, I took off for third. I turned to look at the play at first and saw the ball sail over the first-baseman's head and down the right-field line. Seeing this, I immediately broke for the plate. The first baseman, a big heavy-set fellow, had to chase the ball, pick it up cleanly, turn and throw a perfect strike to the catcher in order to nail me at the plate.

Halfway home, I looked up and was shocked to see the ball being thrown toward the plate. How did the big first-baseman track the ball down so fast? The ball beat me and the catcher had the plate completely blocked. My only chance was to barrel into him and hope to jar the ball loose. With a full head of steam I smacked my wiry body into the fully padded catcher. We both fell hard to the ground in a cloud of dust. The umpire waited a split second before making his decision. The catcher held on to the ball and the game was over.

There I lay supine and motionless. Tears flooded my eyes—I was hurting all over. When I realized the wind had been knocked out of me, I crawled onto my knees gasping for air. Everyone ran toward me. The jubilation of North Highway ceased for a moment to make sure I was breathing. I was helped to my feet and joined the rest of my team on the dugout bench. I was too angry and embarrassed to look up at anyone. A few of my teammates came over to me to ask me if I was all right. I just nodded and stared straight down. North Highway players then came into our dugout to shake hands. The usual "nice game" was exchanged among all the players except for their second-baseman who said to me:

"Are you the guy who made me dive and dirty my uniform?"

I felt like kicking him in his athletic supporter.

The coaches praised us and told us to be proud of our accomplishments. Later on, our third base coach asked me why I didn't hold at third. I told him the percentages of throwing me out on a play like that were 100 to 1. He then said that he gave me the sign to hold up at third. I now knew what he meant. I ran through a stop sign. I felt terrible. I admit that I didn't even see him during the entire play. He was there, no doubt waving his arms and shouting to stop. But the intensity of the play carried me away. What was worse, I was then reminded that Brian was due up next—he was batting .500 in the series.

I always knew that this would make for a great story to tell my children and grandchildren. The point is that under normal circumstances, experience breeds maturity and that even as a little-leaguer on that all-star team, we were able to think positively without much outside encouragement.

My father couldn't have been thinking of the Warriors when he said that on any given day, any team can beat another.

It poured very hard in the mid afternoon. Deep down I was hoping the game would be rained out. But that would only delay my decision whether to continue incorporating Grainy Beach into my schedule or not. I needed a couple more ball games to help formulate which way to turn.

In the pregame meeting between the managers and umpires I overheard our manager say:

"Who's the home team? We're up first so we must be the home team." With statements like that, no wonder we couldn't win a game.

In the dugout we waited to hear the starting lineup. When Big Mike didn't hear his name called, he went into a fit of rage.

"I've got an anatomy final tomorrow, and I came down to play some ball. I'm not going to waste my time sitting on the bench when I could be studying."

If the exam was so important to him, why didn't he stay home altogether? He continued his diatribe despite being told to cool it:

"No, I've been diplomatic all season so far. Now I can't take it anymore. The manager sucks—why doesn't he take himself out? He hasn't had a hit all season."

Sounds familiar? He voiced himself in full view and earshot of the umpires and members of the other team. Any semblance of a team that may have existed before the lineup was made known had now fallen apart. The outburst was demoralizing and very embarrassing. I felt like telling Big Mike that this game was not worth my time, and that he could take my spot in the order. Knowing him, he probably would have said okay, so I kept my mouth shut.

The game picked up on the same note from which the pre-game activities had started. We were behind 3-0 after two innings and it looked like we were going to suffer another beating. The team we were playing had some powerful hitters; with an effortless swing, the ball would fly off the left-field fence. But we came back with two runs in our half of the inning. They then went ahead 4-2 on a home run and then two innings later 5-2 on a bases loaded walk to the guy who homered his last time up. In the sixth inning, in amazing fashion, we tied the game mainly on walks. Could we actually win one?

This see-saw contest drained our emotions. But we began to think that luck was on our side this time. Though before we could cherish the thought, the very first pitch served to them in the top of the seventh was lined over the left-fielder's head for an inside-the-park homerun. That killed our momentum. What burned me up about the play was that Tom was playing too shallow despite being told to move back. He dared the hitter at the team's expense. The ball was otherwise catchable. Once again Tom's inability to act as a team player destroyed any chance of our winning the game. I was beginning to take it personally, since I was the one who told him to play deep. They added another run shortly thereafter. That closed out the scoring for the game.

My usual post-game analysis included the following statistical insight - we scored 2.5 times as many runs as our first three-game total. What's the significance of this stat? It would seem to indicate high confidence levels as a result of a new rank (batting) order; however, no direct correlation exists thus disproving the (null) hypothesis which theorized that the Warriors are in the midst of understanding their regression. Simply put, there is no significance. We did hang tough against a strong hitting team, but again we were outclassed. Since this was our fourth loss in four games, I was able to observe first-hand how losing builds character. And let me tell you, we've got some real characters on this team.

If one looked hard enough, some semblance of team cohesiveness was evident, but with outbursts such as those displayed by Big Mike, it was difficult to reinforce. You may think that when there is one deviant, the rest bands together against him to demand his ouster. But nobody took a stand because, though insensitive, the logic of the "deviant's" arguments about not starting was well-founded and downright correct. For example, "the manager sucks" was impeccable logic.

Before we departed for the evening, we were reminded of next week's double-header. Immediately two guys said they couldn't make it. That left only eleven to fight for ten starting slots. Maybe Big Mike would start next week. I already made up my mind that unless things changed drastically, this would be my last week in the league. The mystique of Gerald's team I've been hearing about over the last two years kept my curiosity at a high enough level to wait it out for one more week. The anticipation of finally playing against knowns was also something different to look forward to. Either way, it would serve as the critical point in the season. Gerald's team was 1-3 after today, so that gave us some hope for salvation. The only thing that would have convinced me to stay on beyond next Sunday would be an 8 for 8 day at the plate and a sweep of the double-header. Since I raised my batting average 143 points last week, there's no reason why I couldn't raise it another 457 next week.

You've got to admit; dreaming does have some redeeming features.

CHAPTER SEVEN

NO TWO WAYS ABOUT IT

During the week I received a phone call from Yank, a friend who was playing in a softball league at Floyd Bennett Field. This was the site of Brooklyn's first airport named after Floyd Bennett in 1931. He was a famous American aviator most noted for his piloting the first successful flight over the North Pole and for demonstrating the feasibility of scheduled airline operations. Having failed as a commercial success due to its distance from the city, the airfield has been used mainly for private purposes by the U.S. Naval and Marine Aviation Corps, the Coast Guard and the New York City Police Department. Softball lines and bases were painted onto the airfield's runways apparently to provide recreation for those who trained while based at this location.

I had actually heard from Yank a few weeks ago. He asked me if I would be available to be a fill-in on his team when they were short a player. I said I'd be delighted to. Since I hadn't heard from him in over a month, his call caught me by surprise.

"Hey guy, how would you like to play ball with us this Sunday?"

"Uh, I don't know. What time?" I asked.

"Game time is at 10am. We play two—figure until about 1pm."

"Well, let's see. I've got a double-header that evening. I can't remember ever playing four softball games in one day. I'm not seventeen years old anymore, you know."

"We could really use you. One of our guys had to quit the team for personal reasons and we have a slot to fill."

"Was it your shortstop?" I asked with hopeful anticipation.

"No, but if you want to play short, you could alternate with Pomerantz, who's pretty solid. Otherwise we'll work you into the infield somewhere."

"All right, I'll come. Why not? How many chances will I have to play four league games in one day?"

"Good. If you have the strength, the time or both, you can join us on a regular basis."

"Let's take it one step at a time. I happen to be reevaluating the other league I play in because the evening games turn out to be really inconvenient. It kills the day. Playing in your league makes more sense. I'll come this Sunday, see how it works out."

"You know where the field is?"

"I know where the airfield is, but where are the softball fields?"

"Right on the runways".

"Come on, you're not serious?"

"I'm not joking. You'll see. Actually, it is complicated to explain how to get there. Why don't you meet me at my house and you'll follow me?"

"Sounds like a plan. What time?"

"How's 9am? We'll need some time to warm up."

"See you then. Take it easy."

What, am I crazy? Getting involved in yet *another* league? Next thing you know I'll also be playing in the error-laden league at 8am. (In actuality, I bumped into one who frequents that league; he asked me where I've been lately. All I needed to rekindle the spark of playing for them was that one little innocent question. I resolved to make an appearance at their next game—but not this coming Sunday—please). Well, crazy I'm not. This Sunday will yield more results than I expected. There was a certain amount of unexplained anticipation attached to knowing that I will be in total control of making earth-shattering decisions to either leave one league and join another, join a third league, or play for none of them. I could hardly wait for Sunday to come.

It was a bright sunny morning. A mild chill was in the air, but that would soon dissipate into the warm rays of the sun. I met Yank and I followed him on the Belt Parkway to Flatbush Avenue South and continued along toward the Marine Park Bridge which separates Brooklyn from the Rockaways and Queens. For about two and a half miles we were flanked by golf courses, tennis courts, marinas, driving ranges, Toys-R-Us, and finally the vast open space of Floyd Bennett Field.

We had to drive the complete length of the airfield from the outside in order to get to its entrance right before the bridge. We passed what was once the security guard post and then made a sharp left along a narrow, winding road to get to the perimeter of the airfield. We then drove passed what appeared to be boarded-up buildings, old barracks, and large airplane garages, where there was some activity. Weeds and dried out grass sprouted everywhere, even through the crevices in the road and on the sidewalks. A right turn and a sharp left around a central administration building brought us to a wide open space. Parking spots were available in front of the building. We got out of our cars and were immediately hit with a very strong wind; it was so strong, my hat flew off a distance of fifty feet and I had trouble keeping my eyes open. The only other time I experienced such a wind was standing on the outside terrace of the 86th floor of the Empire State Building. I couldn't imagine playing ball under these conditions.

"Is it always this windy?" I asked.

"Not like this", said Yank. "There is usually some wind due to the open area and being right off the water. But this is the worst I've seen it in a while."

"Where's the field?"

"Out there."

"Out where? I don't see any backstops or boundaries."

"You'll see the base paths, bases, and foul lines outlined in white paint once you get closer."

This was truly wild. I've played on makeshift fields before, but the airfield literally blew my mind. The irony of it was that the ten (yes, ten) fields were not makeshift at all. They were all well-designed and evenly marked. The only negative was the lack of artificial boundaries. So for example, the team that was at bat had to put up a back-up to the catcher in case of a wild pitch or foul ball. The outfielders could play as deep as their hearts desired to ensure that no fly balls sail over their heads. Once a ball does pass an outfielder, though, it's "forget it time". One could run an entire marathon chasing fly balls and worse, foul balls down the lines in right and left. On some occasions, the ball went so far down the airfield, we had to track it down by car!

Batting and fielding practice was a scream. With the wind swirling in all kinds of directions, we never knew which way the ball would travel. The wind would also make it noisy—in order to hear a teammate across the diamond, one had to shout. Routine fly balls would become real adventures; a pop fly to second base would end up in foul territory off the third base line. Throws to first would arrive there on the tenth bounce. A check swing would take the ball to deep left field. The wind would make weak hitters look powerful, and strong-armed infielders look frail. It all depended on which way the wind was blowing and what position one was playing at the time.

Pitching was just as unpredictable. Controlling the ball was difficult, to say the least, and it made for some very interesting pitches. One pitch coming straight at my head broke back across the plate for a strike. The umpires must have seen every conceivable pitch thrown to a batter. It took a while before he knew just what he was calling. We heard many b'strikes and st'balls.

In one game, I was scheduled to bat seventh for the Pilots and play second base. Even though I knew only one guy on the team before I came down for the first game, I felt like I fit in with the rest right from the outset. Most of the players were in their upper twenties and thirties and had a refreshing down-to-earth quality about them. Non-critical, unassuming and supportive is the way I would describe them. A far cry from the crew from the Warriors. The Pilots naturally bonded well together in this league that was comprised of teams made up entirely from one ethnic group. It was interesting to see an all African-American team go up against an all-Irish team, and a practically all Jewish team face an all-WASP team. Today's game was every bit of the latter.

We were playing a team sporting names such as Redmond and Dormody. They were young, had short tempers, and had that look in their eyes with alleged intent to impale our team onto a pole if they could.

The game started out rather innocently. They scored first on a couple of bad breaks and had a 3-0 lead in the second inning. I came up with the bases loaded and promptly lashed a single to right knocking in two runs. We tied the game 3-3 going into the fourth inning. We began to realize that the wind was affecting the opposing pitcher. Our captain instructed us not to swing until a called strike was thrown. Our patience paid off as we were getting some walks, but we couldn't cash in with that timely hit. Meanwhile, they scored six unanswered runs in the next two innings. Nothing went our way—they found every conceivable hole in our infield and outfield. We had to do something; it was the last inning already.

We decided to be more patient than ever. We all took two strikes before we would attempt to swing the bat. This time it worked—we got men on base and got the pitcher to groove a couple. One of their players, who was sitting on the sidelines at the time, called us a bunch of pussies for not swinging. We didn't know it at the time but he was anxious to get the game over with so that he could pitch against us in game 2. He got so angry at one point that he threatened each batter and dared anyone to shut him up. It was disturbing, but we succeeded in scoring three runs to pull within three at 9-6. With two outs now and runners on second and third, I came up to bat for the fourth time. I was 1 for 3 with two RBI's to that point. I took two strikes and ran the count to 1-2. The next pitch was going to be a strike, so I swung hard and lined it between first and second. I thought for sure it would be a base hit, but just as nothing else went our way, their second-baseman extended himself fully and the ball lodged itself in the webbing of his glove. We lost the game, but set ourselves up beautifully for the next one.

We knew we lost on bad breaks—not on poor play. Our confidence stood strong especially when we saw "Mr. Pussy" warm up on the mound. He was now going to get a taste of bitter medicine from closer range. We held to the strategy of taking two strikes. He promptly walked the first three batters. His impatience already started to eat him up. He yelled and ranted and raged at the umpire, his teammates, the batters, and at himself. He then tried to slip a fastball by our number four hitter with an 0-2 count on him. The ball sizzled down the left-field line and continued rolling for two miles down the runway. The grand slammer was quadrupley delicious. We were delirious with laughter as we watched the pitcher hear us saying "Look who the pussy is now!"

That was just the beginning. Four runs in this wind weren't enough and we knew it. We then started to swing before two strikes because the pitcher was convinced by now that he had to throw the ball over the plate. And we made him pay dearly for it. We batted around twice in the top of the first and scored 14 runs. He was so embarrassed and embarrassing as a result, his teammates started to get upset at him. Since there was no hole to crawl into, he had to bear it and stand on that mound and try to get three outs. The law of averages caught up to us, but we didn't mind leaving men on base with a 14-run lead. It was by far one of the most satisfying innings I've ever had. Mr. Pussy was relieved of his duties on the mound and limbered toward left-field. His head hung in disbelief. We didn't hear another word from his foul mouth for the rest of the afternoon.

They started to make a comeback with the score 18-1. In the fourth they scored five runs and thought they were on their way to catch up. One could see it on their faces as they gave it the good ole college try. They wanted to inflict some damage upon us. But it was too little too late—we romped 23-6. I was 1 for 4 again with two RBI's and a walk before leaving the game early for a replacement. Why risk injuring a talent in a blow-out, right?

The day turned out to be sunny and warm indeed. Of course, I didn't feel that until I drove back to civilization. There, a strange sense of serenity pervaded the air. It was nice to get out of the car without having the wind smack you up against the door handles.

I rested the next three hours. At 4:30pm I left for the Harry Maze Field on East 57th Street off Avenue D to join the awful Warriors. We played on this field last week—maybe it would work to our advantage. There were lines of double-parked cars alongside the park. As I drove to the middle of the block, two guys dressed in red uniforms were standing in the middle of the street blocking my path. Naturally, I stopped the car. After sitting on the hood of my car for a long moment, Gerald and Mike came around to my window and greeted me with enthusiasm.

"Hey guy, what's doin'?" Gerald began.

"Where am I supposed to park around here?" I asked.

"There's a game going—as soon as it's over, it'll clear out," Mike answered.

As I took the car around the corner, I reflected on the short exchange that just took place. This was the first time I actually enjoyed coming to play. It makes a big difference to be amongst friends versus mere acquaintances or less. Even if you have a losing record, a long-time friend helps you put things into perspective. Somehow the time passes by easier and a sense of belonging keeps the attitude on a positive note. I wish I had such a friend on the Warriors. Aside from Andy, I felt aloof and estranged from the rest.

I found a spot towards the corner and parked. I wasn't quite sure how safe it was there, but I tried not to think about it. The double-parked cars started to thin out as the last out of the game was recorded. I approached the field as my teammates scattered to their positions for batting and fielding practice. I grabbed a bat and was second in line to take some cuts. Having done so, I trotted out to right-field. The sun was blinding out there. All I heard was the crack of the bat—I couldn't spot the ball until I saw movement from other players. I did manage to see Curt running toward home-plate from center-field. Since I didn't want to become blind before the game started, I moved over to center to shag some flies. Gerald came out onto the field and kept me company. Shortly thereafter more of his team came onto the field than mine, but I stayed out there as we were already in the middle of a highly profound philosophical exchange:

"You know", I said, "my team is really in bad shape. We can't do anything right. And when we can't do anything right, we all get on each other. And when we all get on each other, we can't do anything right."

"Sounds like your team is in bad shape." Gerald noted.

A lazy fly ball came our way.

"I'll take it", I shouted.

I took a couple of steps in and perched my glove under the down-flight of the ball. As it drew closer, I adjusted my feet to get in position to throw the ball back to the infield. Suddenly, Gerald stuck his glove above mine (he's 6'3"—I'm 5'7") and snatched the ball before it could hit my glove.

"You should have jumped", he said.

No sooner than he finished his sentence, did another fly come our way.

"Jump, jump!" he shouted with glee.

I had to run a few feet behind as the ball carried well. I tracked it down—after it stopped rolling.

Another ball came our way. I was still in deep center, a good twenty feet behind Gerald. The ball was closer to me than to him, so I had an easy one finally.

"My team isn't any better", Gerald said matter of factly. "You see that guy over there? He's got the biggest mouth on this side of the Mississippi. And that one taking practice swings—he tries to tell everyone what to do all the time. Our manager takes everything too seriously. He's running the team like we were in the f__'n army. He's taken all the fun out of the game. I'm not enjoying this season at all. And on top of everything, I hardly get to play. I was their best hitter last year and now, since I haven't gotten on track yet, I'm being benched. It's ridiculous!"

"Yeah, it's the 'what have you done for me lately syndrome'. So if you're not having a good time, why don't you just bow out gracefully?"

"I really think I will. I've been thinking about it a lot lately. I'm going on a trip to China for a few weeks and then have to tend to some other commitments—so it's not like they are going to miss me—I wouldn't be playing anyhow."

"If I were you", I said, "I'd take myself out of this misery today. What about Mike?"

"He's the only decent catcher we've got. Besides, he's really into the seriousness bit with the rest of them. The guy at the plate—he's probably the best center-fielder in the league. I've never seen a guy run so fast in my life. He's like really incredible—he catches everything in sight and beats out grounders to the infield. On top of that, he's a real nice guy—the only other one I could really talk to on the team."

"So you're serious about quitting?"

"I'll have to see. It's the attitude I don't like. I want to come out on a Sunday and have a good time, but taking the game seriously at the same time. My team has a sense of humor of zero. There's a lot of pressure put on you. If you make an error or strike out, you get yelled at. Who needs it?"

"I feel the same way" I said. "As a matter of fact, I've decided to call it quits after today. Also I got an offer from another team."

"Oh yeah, which one?"

"Didn't I tell you? They play out in Floyd Bennett Field. A friend of mine asked me to come fill in for someone. Today was my first day there—and they saw what a great talent I am, so they asked me to join them."

"They must be desperate" murmured Gerald.

"I'll make believe I didn't hear that. Anyway, it's wild out there. The wind swirls like crazy. You're in the middle of a runway with no protection whatsoever. If you're up at the plate with the wind at your back, the ball carries forever. It made for some very interesting plays this morning."

"How'd you make out?"

"We lost the first game 9-6, but mauled them in the second 23-6."

"Get any hits?"

"I went 1 for 4 in both games and drove in a couple of runs in each game."

"Did you get to play shortstop?"

"Yes, in game 2. I made one bad error. Throwing to first was an adventure. You never really knew where the ball was going to end up. But it was fun. The guys there all had the right attitude. They rewarded you for doing well, and didn't get all over you if you messed up. That's the way it should be."

Just then the umpires called for the start of the game.

"How many homers are you going to hit today?" I asked.

"Five in the first and four in the second game."

"Maybe when the Messiah arrives."

We parted to our respective dugouts. Having a normal dialogue in this setting felt good. But now it was back to morbid city for the next two hours.

At game time only nine guys from our team showed. Even Squiggy didn't show—he was a guy who looked like the character Squiggy from the popular Laverne and Shirley television show. He came to every game disheveled and bombed out of his mind. To this day I don't know which player he came to watch.

If I recall correctly, the league rule stated that if at any time less than nine players show up, the team would not only forfeit the game, but would be kicked out of the league entirely. Maybe we should have put ourselves out of our misery. Lenny came over to me and thanked me for showing up. He said he tried to get in touch with me during the week to make sure I could make it today because he knew only eight were coming without me. Only then did I realize why he was relieved when he saw me.

Imagine that. The team's continuity rested on my coming or not. What if I weren't playing Gerald's team today? I may not have shown up at all. I would have called Lenny to tell him, of course, but the point is he may have been stuck with eight. Fate had it for the misery to be prolonged.

Too bad Big Mike didn't show—he may have actually had a chance to get into a game.

Andy finally had a crack at starting. By this time his sole purpose in showing up was for Amy. Imagine driving to Brooklyn from New Jersey on a Sunday evening just to play softball on a losing team. There had to be more incentive than that. And the way he felt about Amy was plenty motivation. We had talked a number of times about mustering what it would take for him to win her over. It was just a matter of timing. And this was going to be the day that he would make his move. It would be even sweeter than that, because I also had a few choice words that I wished to impart to Tom.

The right-field sun was blinding. I was hoping no one would hit the ball my way. Unfortunately they did. The first one hit to me I managed to catch. I saw spots for the rest of the game, though. The next two were hit fairly high and I lost both of them in the sun. One went for a single; the other, a triple. The single was hit just beyond the second-baseman's position. At first, I thought he was going after it, but he couldn't see it either. It ended up dropping between us. It would have been a double, but there was a runner on first at the time.

The triple was hit deep to the fence in right-center. I got there and had it all lined up, but at the last moment I lost it and it landed right behind me. I was lucky it didn't hit me on the head. It cost us a couple of runs, though.

In the dugout during our half of the inning I noticed that Stevo, Nick and Tom were all wearing New York Mets baseball hats. I asked Stevo about it. He said they went to cap day at Shea Stadium.

"How did you get back so fast?"

"Oh, we left after the fifth inning in order to get here for game time."

Any one of three things could explain this:

1. They were dedicated to the Warriors
2. They knew that if they didn't show, we wouldn't have nine to play
3. They weren't too bright

We were trailing in the game by a couple of runs when they had another rally going. With a runner on second and one out, the batter lashed a frozen rope to me in right. I took it on one hop and fired a strike to the plate and nailed the runner by three feet. Nevertheless, they went on to score four runs—by the time the inning was over, my assist from right-field was forgotten.

In the sixth inning, down 9-3, we scored two runs. In their half of the inning they added another two but not before the defensive play of the game was made (by me, of course). They had a couple of runners on base with less than two outs and a right-handed power hitter at the plate. I positioned myself deep and towards the gap in right-center. The batter took a full swing and popped the ball in the air directly over the right-field line in shallow right-field. The ball was well beyond the reach of either the first or second baseman, so it was up to me if the play was going to be made. In that split second it reminded me of a similar opportunity I had on a wet field a few weeks back during practice before the game.

I got a good jump on the ball and ran full speed at a 45 degree angle from where I was originally positioned. My cap flew off and I sensed a fence coming near. Just before I reached the foul line, I grunted and stretched out; I caught the ball in fair territory as my momentum took me into the fence. I braced myself, whirled, and pegged the ball into second base. The applause from the opposing team was immediate and loud enough for all to hear. "Nice catch!" "Great play!" "Good hustle, right-field!" Only one person (Lenny) from our team acknowledged the play. After the last out was made, while on my way to the dugout, I got some handshakes from the other team. Gerald, who didn't start, was inserted in the last inning into right field. As we approached each other, with a wide grin on his face he signaled for a high five. I obliged. In the dugout, however, there was silence. So mired in the pending 11-5 loss, nobody was capable of appreciating a good play when they saw one. Tom even went so far as to comment that it was no big deal. Not only was I disgusted, but I'd had enough of Tom.

I didn't think I was so insecure that I absolutely needed my teammates to pat me on the back for every good play I made. But we all need and expect some kind of acknowledgment from time to time, and especially after an exceptional play. So yes, I wanted it verbalized in clear, concrete terms. I needed that handshake or slap on the backside. Instead, my teammates just sat there gazing into space; one or two brushed by me to sit at the other end of the dugout. I received zero recognition.

I found myself sitting on top of the back of the bench, incredulous at the lack of team spirit. Even as I sit recollecting this event, I cannot understand how practically an entire team can just ignore the fact that a super catch was made before their eyes and not appreciate it. Could it be that it was the 11-5 score that kept their enthusiasm down? Was it me, the elder-statesman that could possibly have caused jealousy? Did the catch legitimize me as a solid ballplayer, thus placing a threat to others by moving in on their position in the next game? I had no answer.

Hearing Tom's words about the catch not being such a big deal, I turned and said in full earshot of the entire team, including Amy:

"Who the hell asked you for your usual stupidity?"

"What did you say?" as he brought his grimy face closer to me.

"You heard me" I said.

"Well, I'm gonna kick your butt in after the game."

"Is that the only way you know how to express yourself? Wanna prove to everyone how badly you can lose in a fight?"

At this point Andy was poised to jump in and defend me since all the rest were silently siding with Tom. But I was confident that even if I got hurt, I would get my licks in no matter what. More importantly, Amy began to see Tom's true colors for the first time. His masterful cover-up was now to be short-lived.

Before Tom could raise a finger, Lenny stepped in and cooled us both down. If only for the moment.

True to Gerald's word, his team displayed the intensity he described earlier—even with a six run lead in the last inning. They had a 1-3 record to date and were desperately trying to get to .500. They knew they were a better team than their record showed, and wanted to prove it. It was admirable to a point, but at times got out of hand. For example, at the outset of the inning, Lenny's brother was sitting up against the fence on the field side of our dugout for a better view of the game. He was a few feet behind our first base coach, well in foul territory, and not in anyone's way. Technically speaking, nobody should sit there, but we're not talking major leagues here. Their first-baseman called time, pointed a finger at him and told him to go inside the dugout. He said it with such conviction you would think he was blocking his view of the game.

I couldn't hold myself back from yelling out:

"But he paid good money for that seat."

This prompted others on our team to respond in kind to the first-baseman:

"What's it to you?"

"He ain't botherin' no one."

"Who do you think you are, the ump?"

Alas, some life! The umpires saw to it that he was safely in the dugout before play resumed. Echos of boos at their first-baseman ensued. The 11-5 loss didn't bother me—I was having too much fun getting on the first-baseman.

The sun began to set and right-field was a pleasure in game 2. It was a rather uneventful game, but I became more verbal than in any other game because this was to be my last game on this team and only I knew it. I started to wonder what excuse I would give for quitting the team. Maybe I would say that the time of day is not convenient for me and my family. Or maybe I would say that I am going away for the summer. Perhaps that my boss is sending me on an extended business trip abroad.

How about if I just told the truth? That I can't stand playing on a team that is lifeless, hitless, wifeless, and witless. I'd need a couple of more days to figure this out. Meanwhile, I was to give no indication at the end of the game—which we lost 6-0.

A team meeting did not take place after the game. Everyone would have scattered away quickly, except Tom and I had some business to finish. But it never materialized. After the last out I heard him shout over to Amy: "Hey Amy, get the f- - over here." The inevitable then happened. He couldn't hide his natural uncouthness and crude demeanor forever. Before a shocked Amy could respond, Andy jumped in to her defense:

"What did you say to her?" as he brought his face up close to Tom's.

"What's it to you?" said Tom.

"That's no way to talk to anyone. Where do you come off talking like that?"

"Why don't you just mind your own business?"

"I'm making this my business, pal."

"She's my girl", said Tom, "and I could say anything I want without having to check with anyone—especially you!"

Amy's silence could no longer be contained.

"Tom", she called, "you lousy son of a bitch. How could I have been so blind? Now I understand why you wanted me around; just so you could show me off to your friends. You never really cared how I felt about anything. You had to have your way with everything. But it's over now. You could take your entire act and go play with yourself for all I care."

As she turned to storm away, Andy and I caught each other's eye. We both knew what he had to do next. He promptly went after her, placed his arm around her shoulders, and then escorted her into his car. They drove away into the sunset together. What a storybook ending!

Tom went crazy. He began cursing and shouting and was so enrapt in himself, that one by one the rest of the team distanced themselves from him and made their way to their respective cars. Tom completely forgot about me, and seeing what had just transpired, I walked away very much satisfied.

Lenny reminded me about next week's game while I watched Gerald's team being given a pep talk by their manager. They all gave a loud charge cheer for having swept a double-header. I listened in while I waited for Gerald and Mike:

"This is the turning point of the season. We got back on track and won't look back anymore. Now let's put our heads together and get even tougher next week." Another loud grunt in unison. "You guys enjoy tomorrow as a day off—relax and come back refreshed for practice on Tuesday."

They left. The three of us hung around for a while longer.

"Your manager is real sick," I said.

"Yeah, didn't he sound pathetic?" Gerald chimed in.

Mike just stood there smirking. He knew we were right but wouldn't admit it. We then turned to talking about the games.

"You made two great plays in the first game," Mike said to me. "The kid still has it in him."

"Thanks", I said. "Funny thing is that more guys on your team appreciated them than on my team."

"You kidding?"

"No. The guys on my team are a bunch of self-centered individuals who aren't smart enough to know what it means to be a part of a team. It's been really sad to be a part of them."

"How did you get on that team?" asked Mike.

"It's all Gerald's fault. He hooked me up with them."

"Who knew they were going to be this bad?" Gerald said.

"I can't blame you. I had a strange feeling ever since the first practice session back in March. I really didn't like what I saw, but I figured why not give it a shot. I now see that I was expecting too much. They're just a bunch of kids. They really have no business in this league. I wouldn't be surprised if the team doesn't win a game all season. But your team, man, I couldn't see playing for you guys either. During the first game today, your manager was embarrassing someone for making an error. I wouldn't stand for that. What's with him?"

"I don't know. He must have this obsession about coming in first place."

Just then the winning pitcher of game 2 walked over. He happened to have pitched a superb game.

"Nice game," I said.

"Thanks."

It was evident from some small talk that he was "possessed" by his team manager. He left shortly thereafter as did Mike.

I turned to Gerald.

"So, you wanna come by for supper? I'm going to my mother's tonight—I'm sure she won't mind."

"Nah, it's late and I'm tired."

"Walk me to my car and I'll give you a lift back to yours."

"How's the wife and kids"? he asked.

"Why don't you come by more often and you'd see for yourself."

"I will. I've been getting home really late recently from work."

We got into my car.

"So are you going to quit your team?" I asked.

"Not officially. I'll probably just not show up. Is this it for you?"

"Yup", I said. "I didn't tell them yet, though. I have to think of a good excuse. I don't think I could bear telling the truth—it's too painful."

"This is my stop," Gerald said. "How much do I owe you?"

"A visit to my house."

"You're on. I'll call you."

On the way to my parents' house, I played back the events of the day. Four games—one near fight and one definite win. But it was a sweet one. I had a new league to look forward to if I wanted it, leaving behind an 0-6 team with no hope for improvement.

My muscles were aching. But I had dinner at my mother's waiting for me—it would heal all my wounds.

AFTERWORD

One of the skills that I strengthened as a result of being a part of three different teams that spring was my ability to philosophize. I would literally ponder over seemingly meaningless issues and tribulations. Not a day went by when I wouldn't delve into the relative merits of jogging the night before a game or eating at an early wedding on the day of a game. When should I take a haircut? If I'm swinging the bat well and the hat of the uniform fits comfortably over my hair, what will it do to my swing if I take a haircut now? Is it important to wash out the uniform if I didn't sweat during a game? What if the uniform shrank in the dryer? If I miss a Saturday morning practice, should I make it up by going to the batting cage on Saturday night? Or will supplicating in the synagogue give me all the strength I would need to do well the next day?

All of the above concerns were relevant and related. Many players go through periods of slumps during their careers and often wonder what they could do to correct their mechanics. Perhaps the left arm needs to be held higher or the stance opened a bit. Maybe the ball is being released too early or the back is not being bent over far enough. Or, maybe it really was that new pair of underwear or change in laundry detergent; it doesn't take much.

These thought processes branched out to more global issues to which I also gave considerable thought. I began to place into perspective many day to day occurrences involving myself, friends, teammates, and others. It was interesting to note differences in outlooks and attitudes and how they were displayed in varying situations. Passing quick judgments was something I left to the unwise.

In the scientific world, much research has been done observing human behavior and how various stimuli, whether induced or natural, affect it. Studies on classical response conditioning (although its initial research was done with dogs) opened up many avenues of understanding behavior. Hence there are those who will respond to something specific the same way every time, and yet others will respond differently. For example, when Big Mike wasn't inserted into the starting lineup, he would rant and rave and curse. It didn't matter to him that he complained of a bruised knee. Others would consider the bruised knee as a key factor in not starting. Furthermore, problems arise if a player comes to the field and just wants to enjoy himself regardless of the game's outcome versus a teammate who plays to win regardless of whether he enjoys himself or not. Moreover, even those with the same goal in mind have conflicts. For those who play to win, arguments arise as to how to go about positioning the team to win. Likewise for those who play for fun, differences of opinion arise as to the degree of non-seriousness.

There is no question in my mind that the Warriors wanted to win. After all, that's what the Grainy Beach league seemed to be all about. If you didn't come to play to win, you got destroyed. The reason the Warriors took their lumps was because they just *came* to win—they didn't come to *play* to win.

This was due in part to most of the players not knowing *how* to win. We were all individuals standing on the same side of the field posing as a team. Most were either just going through the motions or were trying too hard to display their own talents. Few came prepared to play—and that's how most of the games were lost. Fundamentals, basics of the game weren't adhered to. Instead of hitting a cut-off man, the outfielder would throw the ball to home plate—ironically trying to take the short cut to prevent a runner from scoring. More often than not the throw would not even reach the plate. And when we were on offense, our runners couldn't even reach first base. It was no wonder we couldn't win a game.

In professional sports, many owners and managers will insist that their players conduct themselves with honor on and off the field. Their reasoning is that since the players are in the public limelight, they should be role models for those who watch them perform, especially children. Those who ascribe to this philosophy believe that performance on the field of play has a direct correlation to the player's activities off the field. This is where curfews come from.

Other owners and managers who are diametrically opposed to this view will say to a player: "I don't care what you do off the field—as long as you show up on time and give me one hundred percent during a game. If you want to stay up all night before a game, fine. Just make sure you're sober and ready to perform."

Which point of view is correct? I don't know. This issue transcends sports. Basic rights are involved—the right to privacy, the right to ownership, and the right of the public. If you owned a company, would you care if your employees did drugs and got drunk every night as long as their performance between 9am and 5pm was up to par?

Perhaps the answer to this question becomes clear in an employer-employee relationship. But in a voluntary sports league, who can control the actions of players when they're off the ball field? The answer is: nobody, except the players themselves. Some of the players on the Warriors chose not to exercise the right to self-control. These few literally spoiled the fun for the rest of the team.

On the Wednesday night following our most recent double-header loss, I received a phone call from Lou, who told me he just took over as manager of the team. He heard that I had resigned my position on the team from Lenny. I told Lenny that I had to leave the team because the schedule was eating into my Sunday and family responsibilities too much. The real reason was that I couldn't stand the team anymore.

"I heard you're leaving the team", said Lou.

"You heard correctly."

"Why?"

"Because it was messing up my Sundays and because I wasn't having a good time."

"I know how you must feel. Some other guys also left the team and I'm trying to replace them. My only problem is that I need some uniforms for them. When can I come over to pick up your uniform? We don't live too far away from each other—I could be there in fifteen minutes."

"Hold it" I said. I paid seventy dollars to be on the team and for the uniform. It's mine to keep."

"I'll try to get you the money for the uniform sometime."

"Yeah, sometime. Besides, I really don't want the money. I want the uniform."

"I really need it," pleaded Lou. You know one can't play without a uniform."

"Well, why don't you ask one of the other guys who left the team."

"Look, if it's the money..."

"I told you already, it's not the money. For some strange reason I want to remember that I was once a part of this sorry team."

Lou wasn't too pleased with me.

We were approaching the Memorial Day weekend, and it would be a long summer. I played for the Pilots on the airfield until the end of their season in mid-July, but I longed for an 8am game with the guys in, you know, "the other league."

I would soon get that chance again. Meanwhile, I enjoyed playing for the Pilots. The tone was very much competitive—but there was room for fun as well.

I finally picked a Sunday morning in August to join once again the guys from "the other league." At 8am I arrived at 18th Avenue and 56th Street. As I approached the grass and dirt field, there were many whom I did not recognize. A crop of new players started to come down as some moved out of the neighborhood and others were away for the summer. But enough of the old crowd showed up to let me know I wasn't forgotten:

"Whoa, look who's here! What brings you down to our level these days?" "What happened? Get kicked out of the majors?" "Couldn't stand being away from us, huh?"

Too embarrassed to reveal all the truth, I just said that the other league (note the irony) plays at 6pm and yes, I did miss it here. When asked how my team was doing I simply said we were having a bad season. I didn't feel like elaborating.

Nothing changed. Nobody wanted to choose. The game, once it got underway, featured the standard errors. I was back to where I started. I realized that the grass was not greener on the other side. We all had a good time together; even with the errors there was a semblance of a game. I tolerated the errors. I even tolerated alternating innings playing shortstop to accommodate some other fellow who wanted to play there.

A few weeks later, I had some free time to be alone on a Sunday morning. The brisk October 1985 air kept many indoors. I took a short drive to Kings Bay Field in Sheepshead Bay, parked my car near the entrance gate and started to walk the perimeter of the park. This was the site of the local little league All-Star games back in 1969. It was completely fenced in and locked on all sides. I slowly circled the adjacent practice field; the dimensions looked very small to me now that it was 16 years later. As I kept walking I was impressed by the condition of the playing field. The advertisements on the face of the outfield fences were not those of 1969—they looked a bit more modern. I then gazed upwards at the flagpole in center and stopped as I reached left-field. I approached the fence and stared at home plate. The sun was strong and I remembered it well as the 12-year old left-fielder. I then turned the corner and headed up the left-field line in toward third base. I saw the stands and the dugouts and I could hear my mind playing back the sounds of the parent-filled crowd cheering their children on.

I replayed my bases-loaded single up the middle, and my slide into home plate. "Those truly were the days", I thought, and years from now I still hope to enjoy those flashbacks to 1969 and also reminisce with my grandchildren about being out of my league in 1985.

ABOUT THE AUTHOR

Bernie Kastner, PhD grew up in Brooklyn, New York and is now a psychotherapist in private practice. He is the author of "Understanding the Afterlife in This Life" (Devora Publishing, 2007) and "Masa El HaOr" (Zmanma, 2010). He is in the final stages of publishing two additional books on the subject of what happens to us after we leave this world. Feel free to check out his website at www.drbkastner.com

At age 54, he still plays in a competitive softball league.